The Manager's Handbook

A Practical Guide to High-Performance Management

Alex MacCaw

Author: Alex MacCaw
Editor: Matt Sornson
Cover: Alice Lee
Layout & prepress: Mario Marić

Paperback ISBN: 978-1-7374387-0-0
E-book ISBN: 978-1-7374387-1-7

Visit themanagershandbook.com for more information
and to hear podcast episodes for each chapter.

Table of Contents

Preface   5

Introduction   7

1. Managing yourself   15

2. Hiring & onboarding   59

3. Coaching & feedback   109

4. Working as a team   147

5. Creating & achieving goals   181

6. Information sharing   197

7. Conflict resolution   213

8. Consciousness   233

The highlights   257

Appendix   265

Recommended reading   265

What does it mean to be an executive?   269

GitLab interview:
GitLab's top strategies for a remote-first workplace   282

Remote Happiness   288

PREFACE

Great management is a thing of beauty. In fact, we believe it's one of the most overlooked points of leverage in this world.

Think back to the teacher who had the most impact on you as a child. Perhaps they coaxed you out of your shell and provided you with a safe place to play and grow. Or maybe they cared enough to give you critical feedback that made you sit up, listen, and change your behavior. It's safe to say you'll never forget them; they changed your life.

Great managers are unfortunately a somewhat rarer breed, but if you've ever had one, you'll feel the same way about them. Your manager can have a significant impact on your life, both positively and negatively. They can change the way you look at the world, coach you to overcome obstacles, and hold up a mirror so you can learn more about yourself. Conversely, bad managers can make you hate your job and then, as often happens, everything else.

Our goal is to set a new standard for great management and to help as many people as possible to get there.

Who are we?

This book was written by Alex MacCaw [*alexmaccaw.com*] with help from the team at Clearbit [*clearbit.com*], a tech company based in San Francisco. Clearbit was founded in 2014 with the intention of providing a vehicle for self-growth for all who work here. In mid-2018, our small, hyper-efficient team of 30 hit an inflection point. The company began to scale quickly, and we effectively tripled our team in about a year.

We saw effective management as a way of maintaining our company culture, values, and employee happiness during this period of extreme growth. We received a lot of coaching and help, and we were lucky enough to work with teachers like The Conscious Leadership Group [*conscious.is*] and Matt Mochary [*bit.ly/mochary*]. We also learned a lot the hard way.

Why did we write this handbook?

This handbook represents the best of our collective knowledge of management. We wrote it as part of the internal management training program at Clearbit, with the goal of developing world-class managers. When we realized that other organizations would probably find it useful too, we decided to publish it.

But we can't take credit for this book. It contains no new ideas. We've simply curated them from teachers and writers who have influenced us. We've included links to their work throughout, and in some cases we've reprinted articles in full within chapters or in the Appendix.

You'll notice this handbook is very specific to managing at Clearbit. This is intentional; we felt that generalizing the contents would only serve to water down the message. Not all the tactics we outline are transferable to every company, but perhaps this handbook will influence your organization's own approach to management.

INTRODUCTION

Congratulations!
You've been promoted
into a manager...

You've made it! Or at least that's the common perception in our society. When you head home for the winter holidays, your relatives might still not understand what you do, but at least they'll be impressed that you've got some people "working for you."

So why is that? Why does society place such a value on management? It comes down to power and compensation. Management is associated with calling the shots and, quite often, a higher salary.

In themselves, these aren't great reasons to become a manager though. Associating management with higher compensation and prestige causes a whole host of problems (which we'll get into later) and, once you've been doing it for a while, you'll realize that the best managers let their team make the decisions. Sure, they act as a tiebreaker every now and again, but their team should be driving things.

Management requires wearing many different hats. Some days you're the recruiter, some days the coach, some days the conflict resolver, and some days the tiebreaker. If you can become great at all these things, then the score will take care of itself. Your team will perform, and you will feel a lot of satisfaction from watching them fly.

It's not a promotion, it's a career change

Associating management with higher compensation is a classic trap companies fall into. It changes all the incentives for individual contributors (ICs) who want to further their careers. Now, rather than doubling down on their strengths, they reluctantly move "upward" into management to gain a promotion. What often happens next is you end up losing a great IC and gaining a mediocre manager. Not good!

At Clearbit, there is no such thing as a "promotion" into management. It's a distinct career change. And like any other profession, management requires years of training and practice to get good at it.

You'll notice this is reflected across our compensation structure. We have two parallel tracks for individual contributors and managers, with clear levels and goals. It's quite possible that the ICs on your team are making more money than you; that design is intentional.

What does it mean to be a manager at Clearbit?

Technically speaking, the role of the manager is to drive output by organizing and facilitating people and processes to accomplish a goal.

However, that's such a dry way of looking at the subject. Management is an art, precisely because we humans are such complex creatures. At its heart, management is an act of service. Great managers coach, teach, and inspire their team to become the best versions of themselves.

Management is not for everyone. If you don't thrive on solving people problems, then it's probably not for you. And that's completely fine; being an individual contributor is just as valuable as being a manager.

So why become a manager? We think there are two core reasons:

1. *Finding joy in the leverage of a high-performing team.* If you're doing a good job as a manager, then your team will perform well and achieve things much greater than you alone could accomplish. There's something quite beautiful about a well-functioning team.

2. *Finding joy in your team's personal growth.* Helping individuals on your team find their zone of genius, coaching them, and watching them grow into their full potential—these are all highly rewarding things to be a part of.

As a manager, you now have a responsibility to improve people's lives, career growth, and general happiness. You can have a big impact on how their lives pan out, for better or worse. Great managers realize the importance of the role they play but are humble enough to bask only in their team's success.

The paradox of management

The paradox of management is that the attitude that got you to that position isn't the attitude that will make you successful at it. In fact, the opposite is true. If you try to manage people in the same way as you produced work as an individual contributor, you will fail.

What made you successful as an IC? Probably some combination of hard work and domain expertise. So, when you encounter problems as a freshly minted manager, it can be all too easy to put your IC hat back on and fix them yourself. At Clearbit, we call this "heroing." Sometimes it's necessary, but it's always unsustainable in the long term.

You have to switch focus from yourself to others because you're no longer measured on your output. It's now about the output of your organization.

📖 Mia Blume delves into this topic in So You've Been Promoted: Five Mental Shifts for New Managers [*bit.ly/new-managers*].

How management is different from leadership

The terms "management" and "leadership" are often used interchangeably, but they are actually two distinct things. In short, management is tactical and leadership is strategic.

Management requires dealing with the day-to-day realities of hiring and aligning people, such as one-on-ones, performance reviews, planning meetings, goal check-ins, etc. Leadership means looking forward, compounding value, connecting dots, taking cues from outside the organization, and talking to customers to come up with a vision that you can communicate to the rest of the company.

Almost every management position involves some degree of leadership. As you rise through the organization, the management-leadership time allocation ratio changes in favor of leadership. Senior executives are mostly responsible for managing themselves and hitting their targets, while CEOs are mostly responsible for being leaders. This doesn't mean that leadership is more valuable than management; both functions are critical.

📖 Keith Rabois has written an excellent piece on what it means to be a leader that we have reprinted in full in the appendix: What does it mean to be an executive? [*bit.ly/lessons-keith*]

Why you'll likely fail to scale as a manager

A startup is defined as a small company that scales with unnaturally high growth. As the company expands, it requires different types of talent, and it's an all-too-common occurrence for the company's growth rate to outstrip yours. When that happens, you can get "leveled": a senior manager with more experience is recruited above you.

This can be bruising to the ego, but quite honestly, it shouldn't be. Practically no one is capable of consistently scaling themselves at these speeds. Rather than taking it personally, you should realize this isn't a zero sum game. Adding some new amazing VP above you will only give you more opportunities to grow, lift us all up, and expand the pie.

There is only one way to delay or avoid being leveled, and that is through self-growth. It requires deep introspection, which means being honest with yourself about your strengths and weaknesses, seeking feedback, and being committed to improving. This can be painful, and since our natural instinct is to avoid pain, we often put self-imposed caps on our personal growth ... which results in being leveled.

Don't panic

This all might sound like a lot to take on, and it is! Being someone's manager is a big responsibility and it's important to get it right. However, remember that every great manager you admire once started out right where you are: as an individual contributor who moved into management. With training, practice, and the right attitude, you will get there. And Clearbit will be alongside you, supporting you every step of the way.

This handbook

Let's highlight the skills necessary to be a great manager before digging into each one in more detail throughout the rest of the handbook.

Managing yourself

As they say on planes, you should affix your own mask before helping others. The same goes for management. You need to be healthy, present, and emotionally stable before you can support others.

In Chapter 1, we'll delve into how best to manage your time (your most precious resource), how to create work-life harmony to ensure that you are mentally and physically fit, and how to take radical responsibility for your own life and happiness.

Hiring and onboarding

Every manager at Clearbit is responsible for building out their team. This means that *every* manager also needs to be a world-class recruiter, from sourcing to evaluating and closing candidates. In Chapter 2, we'll discuss how we approach this.

Coaching and feedback

When it comes to working with individuals, we prefer to think of managers as coaches. Great coaches help their trainees grow into the best versions of themselves by holding them accountable, giving them critical feedback, and supporting them through challenges.

In Chapter 3, we'll explore coaching and feedback. We'll look at how to run an effective one-on-one, how to give and receive feedback, and how to create accountability.

Working as a team

Effective collaboration involves running useful meetings and making good decisions. It also involves people trusting each other, especially around keeping their commitments.

In Chapter 4, we explore how impeccable agreements work, the different types of decision making, and how to collaborate remotely.

Creating and achieving goals

Once you have the right team in place, it's your responsibility to align goals with your team's strengths so people are operating in their zone of genius. Creativity is not an assembly line. Great managers set goals, not tasks. They have a macro-managing approach where they determine the direction, but their team drives how they get there.

In Chapter 5, we'll talk about how to set goals, get buy-in, and delegate effectively.

Information sharing

When left unchecked, information sharing decays at an exponential rate to the size of your organization. It's one of the hardest parts of rapidly scaling a company.

There are a number of tactics to effectively spread information and slow down the rate of dissipation, and Chapter 6 will delve into them.

Conflict resolution

Conflicts inevitably arise whenever people work together. The key is to address them head-on with conflict resolution.

Chapter 7 will present a tried-and-tested structure for conflict resolution through clearing conversations. You'll learn how to make people feel heard, and how to navigate the Drama Triangle.

Consciousness

The last step to becoming a world-class manager is becoming aware of your internal state, and adopting a mindset of abundance, fun, playful curiosity — enabling you and your team to persevere as you solve hard problems together.

In Chapter 8 we'll explore what those values mean and how to encourage them in your team.

1. MANAGING YOURSELF

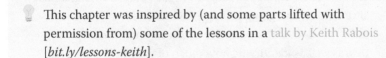 Managing your time & calendar

The first rule in time management is to ruthlessly protect your time. In a world of abundance, your time is the most limited resource. Do not let anyone else create events on your calendar. It should be jealously guarded.

Whenever someone asks for your time, instead of accepting a meeting, ask whether their issue could be resolved with a Slack message, Google Doc, or email instead. If a meeting is inevitable, keep it as short as possible. Ensure that everyone is prepared for the meeting in order to make the most out of the time, and stack your meetings on specific days to ensure long periods of uninterrupted time outside those days where you can get focused work done.

The second rule is to proactively design your calendar.

> 💡 This chapter was inspired by (and some parts lifted with permission from) some of the lessons in a talk by Keith Rabois [*bit.ly/lessons-keith*].

Calendar audits

The first step to proactive calendar design is to understand where your time is already going. This is why Keith Rabois recommends doing a calendar audit and a regular review of your activities and meetings.

"The calendar interfaces we use today actually exacerbate the problem of not optimizing your time. Most executives are entirely reactive to requests for their time and typically let anyone in the organization put meetings wherever they want on the calendar. You should instead view your calendar as something you proactively manage and design. Each Sunday afternoon, write down your top 3 priorities for the week and design your calendar to spend 80%+ of your time on those priorities. You can leave some "leftover" time on your calendar to fill with the reactive requests.

Almost every CEO that we meet with lists recruiting as one of their top 3 priorities. But if we pull up their calendar, most of them have two 45-min coffees and a single 1:1 with their head of talent. If you're only spending 2 hours on recruiting, is it really in your top 3 priorities?

Managing your time proactively is very counterintuitive and not how most people operate. You need to constantly check back in every week to not let yourself slip into a reactive mode and perform calendar audits on a regular cadence. That means sitting down and going through your calendar for the past month and categorizing each event into your various priorities, as well as identifying how much of your time was spent on high leverage activities."

— Lessons from Keith Rabois Essay 3: How to be an Effective Executive by Delian Asparouhov [*bit.ly/lessons-keith*]

To learn how to identify your priorities and then categorize your recent activities accordingly, see Getting things done.

Top Goal

A simple way of ensuring that you get your week's top three priorities accomplished is to block off a Top Goal event in your calendar for an hour every day. You can dedicate this to your most important tasks. Turn your phone on silent, turn off all notifications, and don't check email during this time. See Getting things done for more information.

Spend your time on high-leverage activities

In order to maximize your team's output, you need to spend time on the activities that will influence that output the most. For example, at Square, Keith Rabois would spend at least five hours every week preparing for his presentations at the all-hands meeting on Fridays. That might seem like an inordinate amount of time to spend on a weekly presentation; however, if he was able to communicate a single idea that affected how everyone at the company made decisions, then it was absolutely worth it.

Color coding your time

We recommend using a color coding system when creating calendar events to group activities. For example, use different colors for activities related to recruiting, one-on-ones, recurring sync meetings, customer meetings and time blocks.

This system helps you be more cognizant of where you spend your time, and alter that if needs be. It also helps with energy audits.

Proactively scheduling in recreation

The small joys in life, say lunch with a friend or taking a long walk, tend to get squeezed out of calendars to make way for other people's priorities. It is important to proactively schedule these, otherwise they will never happen.

This is especially critical for exercise. If you are planning to go to the gym on Tuesdays and Thursdays, make sure that's in your calendar (and public to your team), otherwise meetings will replace that time. Make sure travel time is scheduled too.

 "As an introvert, back to back days of meetings are very draining — I avoid them like the plague. Instead, I proactively block off time in my calendar and have meeting-less days to design my calendar to suit my needs."
— *Alex MacCaw*

Energy audits

If you're starting to feel yourself getting burned out at work, it's time for an energy audit (as well as a vacation!). An energy audit is simply looking through your calendar and reflecting on which meetings give you energy, and which take energy from you. Then try to eliminate the latter category by hiring, delegating, and redistributing work.

It is useful to look at energy and leverage at once. Map out activities with leverage on one axis (low to high) and energy on the other (draining vs energizing). High energy, low leverage activities are traps: you really like them, but they should be delegated. High leverage, low energy activities are chores: if you can't automate them, group them with higher-energy activities.

This is also a great exercise to do with your direct reports during their one-on-ones.

♤ On time & present

📖 Matt Mochary, in The Great CEO Within [*bit.ly/great-ceo*], writes about being on time and present. We couldn't say it better ourselves, so here is Matt's chapter verbatim.

It is critical to be on time for every appointment that you have made, or to let the others involved in the meeting know that you will be late as soon as you realize it. This is common decency, yes, but it has a greater importance.

There is someone else on the other side of your agreement to start the meeting at a certain time. They have stopped what they are working on to attend the meeting on time. If you do not show up on time, they cannot start the meeting, but they also cannot leave, because they don't know if you'll show up the next minute or not.

Each minute that they are away from their work is a minute of productivity that you have stolen from them. This is not only disrespectful but also counterproductive. If they are a customer, investor, or recruit, they will not engage with your company. If they report to you, they will keep quiet but resent you. There is no winning scenario when you waste someone's time.

But life happens. A previous call or meeting may run late. Traffic doesn't always cooperate. Even with careful planning, it's not possible to be on time for every meeting. The good news is that you don't need to be.

It is only critical to let the other members of the meeting know that you will be late as soon as you realize that you will be. And you must come to this realization (and let the other attendees know) before the meeting starts, through whatever channel will get to them the fastest. Ideally, you'd let them know about the delay before they have to break away from whatever they are doing before the meeting.

In addition to being on time, you must also be present. Being present means that you are composed, prepared, and focused on the subject matter. It can take a few minutes to "get present"—prepare for the meeting, research the topic and the attendees, go to the bathroom between back-to-back meetings, get a drink or a snack, and so on.

Therefore, I recommend that you plan to arrive at an outside meeting fifteen minutes before it is scheduled to begin. For a meeting in your office, wrap up your current project or previous meeting five to ten minutes prior to the scheduled time for the next meeting.

To make this easy, I recommend scheduling 25 and 50 minute meetings only (Google Calendar even has an automated setting for this). This will give you 5 minutes for each half-hour and 10 minutes for each hour to maintain yourself.

When in the meeting, I often see leaders making the mistake of constantly checking their messages. They cannot get away from being "on," if even for a second. This is not only disrespectful, but it defeats the purpose of the meeting, which is collaboration with the attendees present. It sends a message that the meeting's content is relatively unimportant. Furthermore, it also breeds a bad habit for the entire company—one that will be hard, if not impossible, to break down the line.

During every meeting, leave your phone in your pocket or face-down. Sticking with the strategies of Getting things done will help you to focus on your meetings and make the most out of your assembled—and expensive—talent. And if the meeting is not efficient, then make it so (see Running meetings).

✅ Getting things done

Getting things done, or GTD, is a simple framework for organizing your life and prioritizing effectively. There are many such systems, but they all share two key insights.

1. Your mind is made for having ideas, not for holding ideas. It's a crappy office, and your brain did not evolve to remember, remind, prioritize, or manage relationships with more than four things. Any attempt to do so will cause anxiety.

2. Creative work takes long periods of uninterrupted time. It is disrupted by context switching.

GTD provides space. Invariably, if you capture, clarify, organize, and reflect on all the things that have your attention, it will give you more room. What you do with that room is unique to you. Some people use it to be more creative. Some people use it to be more strategic. Some people use it to be more innovative. Some people simply use it to be present with whatever they're doing.

But I don't need a system

People who don't use such a system have a false sense of control. They will proclaim that their mind is "all they need" to track their commitments, but ultimately they're driven by a deep fear that if they write down every commitment in their lives, they would not only feel overwhelmed by everything, but also feel grief about the amount of commitments they've broken with themselves or others.

You may well feel these feelings, but I assure you that once your system is set up, a sense of relief will wash over you. Have you ever woken up in the middle of the night with anxiety about all the things you have to do? That's a sign that you need to take these tasks out of your mind by writing them down. Your mind can then rest safe in the knowledge that you have a system. You can only feel good about what you're doing when you know what you're *not* doing.

How GTD works

The principles of GTD are very simple. The actual application of GTD is specific to you and your preferred workflow. That said, we've also included some suggestions on which task managers have worked well for us.

These are the steps.

Capture

First, capture 100% of everything that has your attention. Little, big, personal, and professional. Your to-dos, your ideas, your recurring tasks, everything. You want to capture everything so you don't have to think about it again until it's time to do it.

An example of this might be:

* Organize lunch with Patrick

* Prepare a talk for all-hands

* Book sailing-school course

Clarify

For everything you capture, decide if it is actionable. If not, trash it, incubate it, or file it. If it is actionable, and it will take less than two minutes, do it now. Otherwise, delegate or defer it.

Organize

Organize those actionable tasks by category and priority. File them under either *Today*, a list of your tasks for the current day, *Someday*, a list of things that you one day want to do but don't need to get done now (e.g. read a book), or *Defer* to a particular date.

At this point, you may also decide to break up the tasks into various categories. The key thing to remember is not to go overboard; keep things simple. You should be able to understand your priorities for the day in one glance.

Reflect

Look over your lists frequently to determine what to do next. Do a weekly review to bring yourself current, update your lists, and clear your mind.

Engage

Get to work. Choose your next action and get to it. Your system is, at this point, set up to make it easy to figure that out. Your to-dos are organized by priority and placed in categories. Ensure that you have long periods of uninterrupted time for any creative work. Do not get distracted by other tasks, or by incoming tasks (emails, slack msgs, etc.); these can be captured asynchronously.

Using a task manager

We highly recommend using the modern and lightweight Things [*bit.ly/ things-tasks*] to record all of this. While the whole company uses Asana to track commitments between people, we find that this is often too heavyweight for commitments with yourself.

Things has the following advantages:

1. Search. Find all your tasks, attach text files, documents, etc.

2. Scheduled tasks. Push your task out a few days, or to the weekend.

3. Syncing to mobile. Access and capture tasks anywhere.

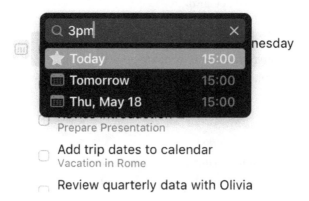

Task managers are so critical that you should feel free to expense any task manager you want to use.

Responding asynchronously

Inefficient people waste a lot of time reaching out about, or responding to, one-off issues in real-time. This wastes everyone's time and introduces a lot of context switching. A much more efficient method is to batch process incoming and outgoing issues.

Throughout the day you will most likely come up with things you want to discuss with your team and others. If someone reports to you, rather than bugging them immediately, consider whether the topic can wait until your next one-on-one. If so, add it to their one-on-one agenda (we use Asana for this). Prompt them to do the same rather than interrupting you throughout the day.

How email fits into GTD

As with any kind of synchronous interaction, email can not only be a huge time sink, but it can also cause you to switch context continuously.

The good news is that you can apply GTD to email fairly simply. The key is to asynchronously batch process your email. Turn off all push notifications and only look at your email twice a day.

Then apply the same principles as above. The capturing step is already done (someone sent you an email), so run through your unread messages and if the response will take less than two minutes, respond right there and then. Otherwise start the message, and potentially use Gmail's delay feature to kick it out to a better time. Then triage your starred messages and get back to an empty inbox.

Email as a stream

The best way I've found to manage email is to treat your inbox as an activity stream, like Twitter, rather than try to read every message. This may not be possible depending on your role (i.e., if it's customer facing), but otherwise I recommend it.

How does this work? Well, you don't need to read every email. Gmail already has a good idea of which emails are relevant to you with its algorithmic importance filter. Here are the steps:

1. Email will flow in. Gmail will automatically tag some of it as important and float it to the top.

2. At periodic intervals during the day (do not enable notifications or respond to email synchronously) check the unread emails tagged *important.*

3. Star the messages you want to keep around, and let the irrelevant ones flow into the stream of emails below. This will train Gmail's importance filter and improve future results.

These are the settings you will see inside Gmail:

General   Labels   Inbox   Accounts   Filters and Blocked Addresses   Forwarding and POP

Streak Settings

Inbox type: Priority Inbox ⬍

Inbox sections: 1. **Important and unread**   Options   ▾

                          2. **Starred**   Options   ▾

                          3. Empty   Add section ▾

                          4. **Everything else**   Options   ▾

Top Goal

In companies, there is a never-ending set of burning fires to attend to, and you can often find that weeks go by and you've achieved nothing. This is the result of getting bogged down with the small immediate things and losing track of the important long-term ones.

The Top Goal framework will help you fix this. Greg McKeown, who wrote a phenomenal book on productivity called Essentialism [*bit.ly/ essentialism-disciplined*], boils this down to one key concept: Schedule an hour each day (that is, put an Event in your calendar) to work on your Top Goal only.

During this Top Goal time, do not respond to emails, texts, calls, and messages. Only work on your top priority during these two hours. If you follow this pattern each workday, you will achieve amazing things.

You should decide on your top three goals for the week during your one-on-one with your manager. By scheduling time to work on your top goal every day, you can make absolutely sure that it will get done.

I'm still procrastinating...

There is no need to feel shame about procrastinating. Services like Twitter, Facebook, and Reddit were literally designed to be addictive and distract you. They're a tax on human attention.

If you find yourself procrastinating, there are two steps we recommend:

1. Build awareness. Install RescueTime [*rescuetime.com*] and track your usage of social media, news sites, etc. Use Screen Time to do the same on iOS.

2. Run an energy audit. Procrastination is often a sign that something isn't quite right. Is it skill? motivation? ambition? Understand which one it is, and address that. It may even be that you like the pressure of a deadline, and you can address that by setting shorter deadlines.

3. Put up barriers between you and distractions. We recommend Go Fucking Work [*gofuckingwork.com*], a Chrome extension that prevents you from browsing social media and other distractions during set hours.

🖌 Coaching

Every world-class athlete has a coach: every tennis player at Wimbledon, every golfer in the PGA, and every batter in the MLB. An athlete without a coach is incomplete.

The sports world figured out long ago that athletes with coaches win. The business world is just catching up.

Great coaches hold up a mirror so you understand yourself better. They provide feedback and hold you accountable. They're a sounding board to debate ideas with, and a shoulder to lean on in hard times.

Coaching for everyone

At Clearbit, we allow any senior manager to expense coaching. If coaching is so useful, why doesn't everyone at the company have an external coach? Well, unfortunately it comes down to cost. At the current size of our business, it's just not viable.

That said, there is an excellent back-up option, and that is your direct manager. Part of great management is coaching, and one of the reasons we've written this book is to turn our managers into great coaches.

Finding a coach

The best way to find a coach that works for you is the same way you find anyone good: ask your network. Failing that, we keep a list of recommended coaches. And finally, we recommend using Torch [*torch.io*], a coaching service.

Advisory board

As the company grows, it is only natural that issues crop up outside of your experience. The worst way to deal with this is to blunder forward, pretending to know what you're talking about. A better approach is to ask for help—and who better to ask for help than a board of advisors.

An advisory board is a set of three to five people who have experience in your domain and have committed to helping you. They are there to answer the odd question over email, pop on the phone with you, and if needed, come by the office. Their networks are also incredibly useful.

An advisory board is a requirement for anyone on Clearbit's leadership team.

 "When I think of how critical advisory boards can be, one example stands out. Clearbit was going through the process of raising venture debt and had been given some conflicting information around the kind of debt we should raise.

I reached out to Patrick Grady, a member of my advisory board, for help. Patrick is an ex-CEO and has raised hundreds of millions in both equity and venture debt rounds, he's seen it all and has a wealth of experience. Patrick not only came by the office to take us through the whole process, but introduced us to an ex-banker who had been on both sides of the table negotiating venture debt. They aided us with the process, reviewed the debt term sheets, and helped us avoid making any mistakes."

– Alex MacCaw

A common objection

Advisory boards sound great in principle, but a common objection I hear to them is: *"Why would anyone help me? Won't they require compensation?"*

Perhaps they will ask for some kind of compensation, but we have found that the vast majority of people are willing to set aside time for you as a way of paying it forward. Every successful person has been helped by other people, and most of them are willing to give back to the community. And a lot of advisors simply enjoy the feeling of creating value. In fact, who doesn't?!

That is one of the very special things about the tech community. Indeed, one day it might just so happen that you too will help some less experienced leader with their own questions.

Setting up your advisory board

Pick three to six people in your network who are either a few years ahead of you in their careers or are semi-retired. Reach out to them, perhaps buy them coffee or dinner, and broach the subject.

We don't recommend opening with any talk about compensation; it changes the tenor of the conversation. It turns out that people feel a lot more satisfaction when they help others out of the kindness of their hearts [*bit.ly/secret-to-happy*].

Contacting your advisory board

We recommend making the barriers to contacting your board as low as possible. One such way is by putting your board into a CRM like Streak [*streak.com*], so that you can easily reach out and customize the email with a mail merge.

 Mental health

Managing takes an emotional toll. It is important that you have someone to speak to, listen to you, and help feelings flow through you. The alternative is bottling up anger, sadness, or fear until you and your relationships self-destruct.

If you can, build a support group of your peers. Learn to be vulnerable in front of your peers and the company. Get therapy. Even if you think you don't need it, you will invariably find it useful.

You are not that voice in your head

Have you ever taken a long shower and had a fictional argument in your head with someone? Or fumed about some situation, letting yourself spiral into a depressed hole? On the surface of it, this is quite silly. You are letting that voice in your head run wild, concocting stories that have little basis in reality.

This voice in your head, the one that tells you that you're not good enough, that you have embarrassed yourself, that someone is out to get you — that voice is *just not helpful*. Do not dwell on it or let it run your life.

Realize you are not that voice. How could you be? That voice is paranoid, jealous, and irrational; that's not you. The very fact that you can observe it means it's not you.

Learning to quiet that voice, and realizing the stories it comes up with are just that—stories—is a key part of mental health. There are a number of tools you can use to quiet it, like therapy, meditation, and The Work [*thework.com*].

Michael Singer delves into this subject in The Untethered Soul [*bit.ly/singer-soul*], a book we strongly recommend.

Meditation

Evidence suggests that meditation is a very good thing for your mind. Meditation helps to quiet that little voice in your head, calm your mind, and improve your focus. Studies show that meditation reduces anxiety, lowers your blood pressure, and improves your outlook on life.

The beauty and simplicity of meditation is that you don't need any equipment. All that's required is a quiet space and a few minutes each day. Start with ten minutes at the same time each day and you will begin to form a habit. Within two weeks, you will experience a noticeable improvement in your mood and stress levels.

There are many forms of meditation, and you should explore them to find one that works for you. We find that, at least initially, a guided meditation app is a great way to get started. We have a team account with Calm [*calm.com*]. Stick an event in your calendar every day to remind you to meditate, and make it public to the company to lead by example.

Therapy

There's a common fallacy that therapy is only for unhappy people; this is not the case. A good therapist will hold a mirror up to you and help you understand why you feel what you feel—a critical aspect to emotional maturity.

We are strong believers in therapy, having personally experienced its many positive outcomes. Think of your therapist as a personal trainer for your emotions rather than a doctor for your sickness. Understanding yourself, your emotions, and your mental habits turns you into a better communicator, a better teammate, and ultimately a better human.

At Clearbit, we offer everyone ten free visits annually with a coach or therapist through Modern Health [*joinmodernhealth.com*]. If you prefer to work with a different therapist, that's fine too—chat with your manager and we'll figure something out.

Therapy for leadership

It's vitally important that anyone with a leadership role is emotionally stable and strong. They are responsible for a lot of people's well-being and growth. That's why we require everyone on our leadership team to have some kind of therapy.

I'm fine, I don't need it

There is a common misconception that therapy is only for ill and/or depressed people. That is just not the case, in our experience. Therapy is a tool for self-discovery, discovering why you feel what you feel, what is behind your behaviors and underlying your actions. Therapists are experts at holding a mirror up to you and prompting you to face your fears.

 "For the longest time I wanted nothing to do with therapy. I was happy, and felt that therapy was only something you should seek if you were sad. On top of that, when I was growing up, talking about feelings or showing emotion was not something encouraged in the household. But I felt like I had a good handle on who I was, and there was not much more to learn.

Oh what hubris! It was only after a series of events completely changed my outlook on life that I decided that, given how wrong I was before about 'knowing myself,' that there was probably more to learn. I found an incredible therapist who has helped immensely with my emotional maturity. Her insights into why I'm feeling what I'm feeling have been crucial to becoming a good leader."

— *Matt Sornson, CMO Clearbit*

Sorry, I just don't have enough time

We all have the same number of hours in the day, so a time issue is actually a prioritization issue. Like meditation, therapy is time well spent. You will actually save time if you are less stressed, emotionally stable, and understand yourself deeply.

 Physical health

Building a company takes a physical toll too which can lead to burn out. All the hard work you put in will be for nothing if the process costs you your health. It is incredibly important that you focus on your physical, emotional, and nutritional health by taking active measures to improve them.

Rather than think in terms of work-life balance, think in terms of work-life harmony. Integrate health into your lifestyle. Go to the gym during the day, if that suits your schedule better, dial in to all-hands if you need to drop your kids off at school, and use our untracked vacation to unwind.

Developing good habits

Developing good habits is the key to health. Getting into habits of regular exercise, meditation, and therapy, to name a few, will give you daily incremental improvements that over time will result in complete transformations.

On the flip side, bad habits will slowly chip away at you. For example, consuming more calories than your body uses won't be noticeable day-to-day, but after a few years you'll look in the mirror and ask yourself: "However did I get so out of shape?"

How are habits formed? It turns out that every habit starts with a psychological pattern called a "habit loop," which is a three-part process. First, there's a cue, or trigger, that tells your brain to go into automatic mode and let a behavior unfold. Then there's the routine, which is the behavior itself. Lastly, there is the reward: something that your brain likes that helps it remember the "habit loop" in the future.

We often forget about the first and last part of habit loops. In order to automate positive habits, it can be useful to create intentional cues and rewards. For example, the cue for going to a Barry's Bootcamp workout could be seeing the event in your calendar, and the reward is the delicious milkshake at the end. Going consistently on the same days each week helps form a habit better than one-off workouts. The more ingrained a habit, the more automatic it becomes.

There are many types of triggers or cues for habits. Your environment is an important one that can set you more up for success or failure. Make sure you have healthy defaults in your life. This means healthy food options, regularly scheduled exercise, etc.

Exercise

All the evidence shows that exercising is one of the best things you can do for your physical and mental health. From longevity to happiness, exercise is the key.

You should ideally take some form of movement or exercise every day, but at least ensure that you're working out multiple days a week. Experiment with what type of movement and exercise works for you, be that weight training, dancing, running, or yoga. Make sure to have a regular cadence by scheduling this ahead of time in your calendar.

If you find your self-motivation is slipping, get a buddy to train with, sign up for group activities (e.g. Barry's Bootcamp), or get a trainer.

Nutritional health

Nutrition is not about dieting or losing weight. Nutrition is about giving your own unique body everything it needs to perform optimally. What you do or don't eat can affect your mood, ability to focus, quality of sleep, and the amount of energy you have to get through the day. Some people are more sensitive to eating processed foods than others. For some, a vegan diet is what works for them, whereas another person would become very sick without having meat in their diet.

It is important to develop the ability to notice how foods interact with your unique body chemistry, become aware of which foods make you feel heavy and which foods give you energy. You may begin to notice that you're drawn to certain foods when you feel a particular emotion or that you seem to be crashing every day at 3 p.m. Most of us have inherited unconscious eating habits from our families and fall into eating patterns based on the pressures around us.

If you suspect that your diet is not serving you, consider working with a nutritionist who is knowledgeable about the way food interacts with the body and can introduce you to better eating habits. You might also choose to consult a naturopath who can offer testing to find out if there are any foods that are causing problems for you.

Sleep

Many of us go through life sleep-deprived. This has huge knock-on effects on our health and happiness. We make excuses to ourselves and we put off investing in sleep, but imagine how great you would feel if you woke up rested and ready for each and every day. Now imagine that incremental improvement over your entire life — it might change its course dramatically!

Do not stop iterating on your sleep until you have perfected it.

Track it

The first step, as with all things, is awareness. How can you work toward a goal if you don't know what your current status is?

There are some great sleep tracking tools out there, like the Oura Ring [*ouraring.com*], EMFIT [*emfit.com*] (which goes under your mattress), Gyroscope [*gyrosco.pe*], and Sleep ++ [*bit.ly/sleepplusapp*]. Everyone in the company has access to our team account on Gyroscope.

Most of these apps will give you a score so you can start to get an idea of what, say, a late night of drinking does to your sleep.

Use a sleeping mask

This is a simple one, but works for almost everyone: use a sleep mask. It'll help filter out light and, once you're used to it, it will give you an almost Pavlovian response once you put it on by indicating to your body that it's time to sleep.

Make sure you get a contoured one that doesn't put pressure on your eyes. We recommend the Alaska Bear mask [*bit.ly/sleepplusapp*].

Calming your mind

We live so much in our heads that it can be hard to quiet the chatter of our thoughts and drift off to sleep. Indeed, the harder we try, the worse it gets. If you relate to this experience, then we have a simple solution.

The key is to distract your "left brain" and lull it off to sleep. We find that listening to podcasts, or Calm's sleep stories [*calm.com*], is a really effective way to do this.

No screens

This is a given, but try and reduce the screen time in your bedroom. Leave your phone and your laptop outside of the room. Ensure that you are using f.lux [*justgetflux.com*], or Apple's built-in Night Shift mode, to shift the colors of your display to the warmer end of the color spectrum after dark.

Lower the temperature

Temperature can have a dramatic impact on the quality of our sleep. It's a key part of what regulates the circadian rhythm that determines when your body is ready to go to sleep and when it's ready to wake up. Your core body temperature needs to drop a few degrees in order to fall asleep, and then stay at a consistent temperature for deep REM sleep.

It doesn't help that we have mostly switched to using foam mattresses, which absorb heat and then radiate that heat during the night, causing us to wake up in a hot sweat.

If you suffer from this, then the solution is a bed cooler. The best one on the market is called a chiliPAD [*bit.ly/chili-pad*], and although pricey, it will pay itself back in time. If you really want to go all out, we recommend a bed called Eight Sleep [*eightsleep.com*], which both self-cools and tracks your sleep quality.

Note: Men especially are often best suited to a colder bedroom.

More sleep resources

We recommend the book Why We Sleep [*bit.ly/walker-sleep*] by Matthew Walker.

 Facing fear

Fear is caused by a perceived threat to our survival, whether that be a threat to our physical body or an imagined threat to our ego or identity. Fear of physical death prompts you to look both ways as you cross the street. Fear of ego death stops you from asking that attractive guy/girl out because you might get rejected.

While the two threats are logically different things, we often have a difficult time telling the difference between the two. This is because real threats to our physical survival and imagined threats to our ego both provoke the same fight-or-flight response.

Fear is experienced in an ancient part of our brains called the amygdala (colloquially known as the lizard brain). This part of the brain is responsible for processing all fear, both real and imaginary, and doesn't necessarily "talk" to the thinking areas of the brain that provide rational thought.

To be fair to our brains, historically, threats to our ego were sometimes shortly followed by threats to our survival. Up until a few hundred years ago, an argument with another human could have easily resulted in them killing you. Or perhaps banished from the campfire to the mercy of wolves. There were some very real consequences!

The truth is, though, these days a piece of feedback from your boss is unlikely to result in your immediate demise, and giving a humiliatingly bad speech at a company party won't result in you being hunted down by a pack of wolves.

Our minds, however, are still in this ancient place; we over-index fear.

Is fear useful?

Fear is useful in the sense of "hey, there's this thing over here that probably needs my attention." However, when we start acting on that fear, and making decisions driven by that fear, *that's* when we start running into problems.

Let's take an imagined scenario and see how fear plays a role in decision making.

Suppose you have an executive, let's call him Tim, who isn't scaling with the company. You know deep down that you will need to replace him with someone more experienced. However, you also want to keep him in some kind of role at the company, and you're afraid that if you bring the subject up with him that he'll immediately quit, throwing everything into chaos. So what do you do?

A fear-based decision would be to kick the can down the road by telling yourself that Tim could improve. Don't be ruled by your fear; you are not being rational. By delaying the decision, you're doing everyone a disservice. A better approach would be to lean into that fear, be vulnerable, and sit down with him. Explain the position you're in, including your fear that he'll quit. You might be surprised—people really appreciate vulnerability.

Fear is a very base-level emotion. It's programmed into us at the machine-code level. When you are in a state of fear, adrenaline starts pumping and your higher brain functions shut down. Fear prepares us to take action, not to think. It prepares us to escape, or even to fight, and in some unfortunate circumstances, to freeze. Notice that there is no mention of complex problem solving, weighing pros and cons, or taking time to process before action. Clearly it's not a great place to be making complex logical decisions from.

Fear as a motivational tool

It's undeniable, though, that fear is a great motivator, or at least in the short term. Throughout history fear has been a weapon in the authoritarian's arsenal to bend people to their will. Even today, fear of "being fired" is the stick most companies use to get things done.

However, these days, using fear to motivate fails for two reasons. The first is that it leaves a toxic waste that builds up over time and leads to distrust, anger, and hate. The second is that the world is increasingly favoring creativity in the workplace, which you simply cannot instill via fear. Fear is an extrinsic motivation; creativity comes intrinsically. Fear doesn't create a learning environment; in fact, it disables learning.

"Fear is the path to the dark side. Fear leads to anger. Anger leads to hate. Hate leads to suffering."

— *Yoda, Jedi Master*

Facing fear

The first step in facing your fears is to acknowledge them. At Clearbit, you'll sometimes hear the phrase "this might be a fear-based motivation, but...". Naming your fears and shining light on them is the first step to approaching them.

Step 1: Realize you are feeling fear

Your body will tell you when it's in a state of fear. The key is to build awareness of this.

Let's try an experiment: think back to a situation where you were really scared, perhaps a car accident, or a public speech to a massive crowd. Think about where in your body you felt that fear. Was it a tightening of the chest? Or perhaps a pit in your stomach? This is how your body manifests fear.

Learning to recognize this feeling will give you a chance to pause and dig in *before* it rules you.

Step 2: Identifying your fears

Really dig into the underlying motivations behind the fear. For example, does it stem from a fear of a lack of control tracing back to a traumatic childhood experience? Or perhaps your fear of a lack of recognition is ultimately rooted in an indifferent father whose attention you were trying to seek?

For some, even realizing that what they are feeling is fear can be difficult. Here, slow down the process. Notice whether there are times you are seemingly overreacting or have a strong desire to leave a situation. Once fear has been identified as the emotion, ask specific questions about the situation to figure out what the underlying worry is. Ask yourself some questions. What does this mean about me? About others? About the workplace? About the world?

Cognitive therapists use a system called the Downward Arrow Technique [*bit.ly/cbt-arrow*] to identify the root of negative thoughts and unhealthy beliefs.

Step 3: Leaning in

Once you are more self-aware of your fears and your fear-based motivations, the next step is to lean into them. This is painful, but know that doing otherwise only leads to even more suffering.

Really ask yourself whether the fear is rational. Is it a fact, or is it a story in your head? If it's the former, is there anything I can do about it today? Is it really that bad in the bigger scheme of things? Writing your fears down often helps to rationalize them. Dwelling on your fears in your head only serves to stir them up into a toxic paranoia.

Some techniques

Negative visualization

Stoics used a visualization exercise they referred to as negative visualization to train themselves to stay calm and free from emotional suffering in the face of adversity.

Contemplate what you have, and then visualize your life without those things. Imagine life without your significant other, or without your job, or without your health, and so on and so forth. Don't just think about it logically, really feel it deep down to your core.

 "Negative visualization is a stoic technique of mentally visualizing that you've lost things you value from your life. In my case, it is not having the company and the ability to learn as much as I have at all. It makes me realize that our total progress on Atrium in many ways exceeds where I thought we would be at the outset. If you had told me in the beginning that we would have made this much progress on revenue and team so quickly, I would have been ecstatic. So the smaller, daily bumps are much more palatable."

— *Justin Kan, CEO Atrium*

First and foremost, this technique makes you quickly appreciate what you have in life: your health, your family, your opportunities, and more. Realizing how blessed you are can put things into perspective.

Second is the ability to set expectations up front and be far more honest with yourself. What could go wrong? How would you handle such scenarios? Can you overcome or plan for them?

This practice is called a pre-mortem in the business world, but the idea is the same. When you prepare for the worst, you are in a better place to deal with disaster if and when it does arise.

Finally, this practice can help you realize that the things that you are afraid of are not as bad as you made them out to be. What if you lost your job? What if you had to move to a much smaller apartment? What if your work turns out to be a failure?

We build up our fears to the point that they are larger than life. Confronting them, and even temporarily experiencing them, can help you overcome such barriers.

This is a great way of putting your life in perspective, realizing how irrational some of your fears are, and also understanding that it wouldn't be *that bad* if some of them were realized.

Accepting your own mortality

You'll notice that some of the most successful people in this world, like Elon Musk, tend to have a particularly fearless attitude—why is that?

One answer is that it's nature; in the same way that some people have a higher pain tolerance, some people have a higher fear tolerance.

However, it also can be a learned trait, the key part being coming to grips with your own mortality. Now, you might be thinking to yourself, this is a book on management—why dwell on such a morbid topic? Well, that's exactly the point; we just don't like thinking about it. Most of us go through our lives in denial, pretending that we're going to live forever.

The earlier you can come to grips with the realities of your own mortality, the more likely you are to put your life in perspective, care about the things you really should care about, and focus on achieving the things you want to achieve.

Steve Jobs said it best:

 "Remembering that I'll be dead soon is the most important tool I've ever encountered to help me make the big choices in life.

Almost everything—all external expectations, all pride, all fear of embarrassment or failure—these things just fall away in the face of death, leaving only what is truly important.

Remembering that you are going to die is the best way I know to avoid the trap of thinking you have something to lose. You are already naked. There is no reason not to follow your heart.

No one wants to die. Even people who want to go to heaven don't want to die to get there. And yet, death is the destination we all share. No one has ever escaped it, and that is how it should be, because death is very likely the single best invention of life. It's life's change agent. It clears out the old to make way for the new."

— *Steve Jobs*

A parting thought

Viagra, valium, and penicillin all have something in common: they were discovered by accident. Fear (in the workplace) is often the fear of making a mistake. Yet mistakes are often where the magic happens.

Realize there is no *right* or *wrong* in your choices; perfectionism slows you down. As we accept that we will make mistakes, that they will not ruin us, that we will be ok, we can then take more risks.

😇 Radical responsibility

We all like to think we're emotionally mature, but we also all like to think we're good drivers. It's hubris to suggest there isn't some growth to do.

The crux of emotional maturity is to take full responsibility for one's circumstances (physically, emotionally, mentally, and spiritually). This is the foundation of true personal and relational transformation.

Now, most people are willing to say, "Sure, I take responsibility for my circumstances. I understand my actions and their consequences." However, taking full responsibility goes far beyond that. It means taking full responsibility for your *emotions* as well.

The truth is that nobody can make you feel anything. Emotions are generated internally. When someone is yelling at you, all they are doing is vibrating air molecules toward your ears. You choose to feel what you feel, be that anger, sadness, fear, etc. That choice is yours.

That is a hard concept to grasp, and an even harder one to live! In today's world, people are "outraged" at all sorts of things. So the idea that you are outraged because you *want* to be outraged can be a controversial one. That's not to belittle the source of the outrage; just know that all the emotions you have associated with any given outrage are your choice.

When you don't take radical responsibility, you rely on blame, shame, and guilt to rationalize your circumstances and feelings and keep the ego intact. Blame, shame, and guilt all come from toxic fear. Radical responsibility means locating the cause and control of our lives in ourselves, not in external events.

Instead of asking "Who's to blame?" ask, "What can we learn and how can we grow from this? What is my responsibility in this?" We should be open to the possibility that instead of controlling and changing the world, perhaps the world is just right the way it is. This creates huge growth opportunities on a personal and organizational level.

The villain, victim, hero triangle

When we are not taking responsibility and we are blaming others (or ourselves), we fall into what we call the Drama Triangle, where we play the villain, victim, or hero—and sometimes multiple roles at once.

Villain

The stance of the villain is "It's all your fault!". Villains criticize, blame the victim, and set strict limits. They can be controlling, rigid, authoritative, angry, and unpleasant. They keep the victim feeling oppressed through threats and bullying.

In terms of resilience, villains can't bend, can't be flexible, can't be vulnerable, can't be human; they fear the risk of being a victim themselves. Villains yell and criticize, but they don't actually solve any problems or help anyone else solve the problems.

Victim

The stance of the victim is "Poor me!" Victims see themselves as victimized, oppressed, powerless, helpless, hopeless, dejected, and ashamed, and they come across as "super-sensitive." They can deny any responsibility for their negative circumstances and deny possession of the power to change those circumstances.

In terms of derailing resilience, victims have real difficulties making decisions, solving problems, finding much pleasure in life, or understanding their self-perpetuating behaviors.

Hero

The stance of the hero is "Let me help you!" Heroes work hard to help and take care of other people, and they even need to help other people to feel good about themselves, while neglecting their own needs or not taking responsibility for meeting their own needs.

Heroes are classically codependent and enablers. They need victims to help and often can't allow the victim to succeed or get better.

In terms of derailing resilience, heroes are frequently harried, overworked, tired, or caught in martyrdom while resentment festers underneath.

Manifestation

The descriptions above are the most extreme versions of these roles, but often they play out as milder versions of these. Often, people stuck in the Drama Triangle will play out a couple of these roles, flipping between them, and have familiar patterns for doing so. Playing in the Drama Triangle for too long can lead you to spiral and even pigeonhole yourself into some global archetype (such as "I am a failure").

The key is realizing when you're stuck in the Drama Triangle: pause, take a deep breath, and try to approach the problem with curiosity.

Side note: Is it ok to hero?

There are often times inside a startup, which by definition has limited resources, that require a hero; for example, when a manager needs to step in to help an individual contributor who's struggling. This is normal—the key thing is to both acknowledge that you're heroing, and understand it's a temporary stop-gap that does not lead to a lot of self-growth.

One of the most profound realizations you can come to in life is the idea that you are a creator. There are two main ways of looking at the world: things happen 'to me', or 'by me'.

 Enneagrams

There are three ways you can grow in self-awareness. One is to become more self-reflective. Actually pause and point the lens of attention back at yourself, as though there was something outside of you looking back at you.

The second way to grow in self-awareness is to create an incredibly feedback-rich environment where the people around you are giving you feedback – – the most direct form of it.

And the third way is to use some kind of personality instrument. You could use a technical instrument like the Myers-Briggs or another personality instrument. We love a tool called the Enneagram because it's like a CAT scan in terms of self-awareness.

What are Enneagram types?

The Enneagram helps you see things about yourself you cannot otherwise see, such as your core motivations, blind spots, communication patterns, listening filters, style of relating to others, and path to maturity.

It is not an exact science. It is not there to pigeonhole people or to be an excuse for bad behavior. It is just a useful framework for understanding yourself and others a little better. And the better you understand someone, the better you can work together.

Typing yourself

1. First take the test [*eclecticenergies.com/enneagram/test*]. This will take about 15 minutes and will reveal your base and wing type enneagrams. Add the result to your profile page in our wiki so others can discover it.

2. Then read the description of your type [*enneagraminstitute.com/type-descriptions*] on enneagraminstitute.com. These descriptions

are more modern and comprehensive than the descriptions listed on eclecticenergies.com.

The nine types

There are nine Enneagram types. People tend to have one dominant type and one minor (wing) type. No type is inherently better or worse than any other; all have assets and liabilities.

These type descriptions come from The Enneagram Institute [*enneagraminstitute.com*].

1 The Reformer

The Rational, Idealistic Type: Principled, Purposeful, Self-Controlled, and Perfectionistic

2 The Helper

The Caring, Interpersonal Type: Demonstrative, Generous, People-Pleasing, and Possessive

3 The Achiever

The Success-Oriented, Pragmatic Type: Adaptive, Excelling, Driven, and Image-Conscious

4 The Individualist

The Sensitive, Withdrawn Type: Expressive, Dramatic, Self-Absorbed, and Temperamental

5 The Investigator

The Intense, Cerebral Type: Perceptive, Innovative, Secretive, and Isolated

6 The Loyalist

The Committed, Security-Oriented Type: Engaging, Responsible, Anxious, and Suspicious

7 The Enthusiast

The Busy, Fun-Loving Type: Spontaneous, Versatile, Distractible, and Scattered

8 The Challenger

The Powerful, Dominating Type: Self-Confident, Decisive, Willful, and Confrontational

9 The Peacemaker

The Easygoing, Self-Effacing Type: Receptive, Reassuring, Agreeable, and Complacent

Enneagrams in practice

Reading the description of your type is a good start, but where Enneagrams really start to shine is using them practically day to day.

Healthy and unhealthy traits

Every Enneagram has a light side and a dark side. It's worth digging into the unhealthy traits associated with your type to see whether you can identify any patterns you've fallen into. You can then start to catch yourself in the future when you see yourself reverting back to these negative patterns.

Interactions between types

We've found the description of each type's interactions [*bit.ly/ennea-combos*] to be a fascinating way of looking at two people in relationship. We suggest looking up your manager's and close colleagues' Enneagram types in our wiki and reading about the relationship between your two types.

Feedback

Different types like to give and receive feedback in different ways. The Enneagram Group has put together a useful worksheet [*bit.ly/enneafeedback*] as a guide on how to give feedback to the different types.

Next steps

Listen to a description about your type [*bit.ly/ennea-oneal*]. Ryan O'Neal has created a beautiful song and discussion around each type.

Exploring the opposite

The Wright brothers [*en.wikipedia.org/wiki/Wright_brothers*] often took two different sides of an argument, debated the subject, then switched sides and debated the opposing argument. As Orville Wright put it, "Often, after an hour or so of heated argument, we would discover that we were as far from agreement as when we started, but that each had changed to the other's original position."

Our stories can lead to suffering

As we go about our day, we all are constantly interpreting the world around us to give our stories meaning. Often we can witness exactly the same events as someone else and yet arrive at completely different conclusions. How is that?

The stories in our head are a concoction of biases, childhood experiences, misinterpreted facts, and much more. A lot of suffering can result if we hold onto these stories too tightly and are committed to being right.

Almost all the challenges we experience arise from us believing we are right about the way we perceive situations, one another, or ourselves. To understand this, pick an issue that you are wrestling with in your life. When you look underneath, can you see your desire to be right about that issue?

The Work

In 1986, Byron Katie was coming out of the depths of a debilitating ten-year-long depression with a life-changing realization:

 "I discovered that when I believed my thoughts, I suffered, but that when I didn't believe them, I didn't suffer, and that this is true for every human being. Freedom is as simple as that. I found that suffering is optional. I found a joy within me that has never disappeared, not for a single moment. That joy is in everyone, always."

— *Byron Katie*

In other words, what was causing her depression was not the world around her, but what she *believed* about the world around her. Katie went on to create The Work [*thework.com*], a simple framework for turning around beliefs in order to alleviate suffering.

Instead of hopelessly trying to change the world to match our thoughts about how it "should" be, we can question these thoughts and, by meeting reality as it is, experience unimaginable freedom and joy.

The four questions

There are four questions you can ask yourself to help turn thoughts around:

1. Is it true? (Yes or no. If no, move to question 3.)

2. Can you absolutely know that it's true? (Yes or no.)

3. How do you react, what happens, when you believe that thought?

4. Who would you be without the thought?

The four questions in practice

For example, let's take the belief that *"John doesn't appreciate my input"* and go through the four questions.

1. Is it true?
"Sure, I remember he interrupted me mid-sentence last Tuesday."

2. Can you absolutely know that it's true?
"I guess there's no way for me to know his true feelings."

3. How do you react, what happens, when you believe that thought?
"I feel angry. My chest tightens. It ruins any meeting that I'm in with John. I've been fuming about this all afternoon."

4. Who would you be without the thought?
"My mood would be lifted. I'd be a lot happier. I'd be able to collaborate with John again and appreciate some of the qualities I love about him."

So you see, instead of hopelessly trying to change the world to match our thoughts about how it "should be," we can question these thoughts and, by meeting reality as it is, experience freedom and joy.

The turnaround

The next step is the turnaround. The idea here is to see that the opposite of your story is at least as true as, if not truer than, your original thought.

For example:

1. *John doesn't appreciate my input.*

2. Turn it around to the opposite: *John appreciates my input.*

3. Turn it around to the other person: *I don't appreciate John's input.*

4. Turn it around to yourself: *I don't appreciate my own input.*

Often we find that deep-seated anger with others is rooted in things we hate about ourselves; it's a projection. Regardless of the cause, these beliefs are causing us suffering. Realizing that you can turn that around will set you free and create lasting shifts in your thinking and your perception of yourself and the world around you.

But doesn't this lead to apathy?

Beliefs are very powerful, and negative ones can lead to a lot of suffering. By turning them around, you can alleviate your own suffering and then problem-solve from a place of playful curiosity.

Treat The Work as a meditation. It's about awareness; it's not about trying to change your mind. Would you rather be right or be free?

A full example of the practice

A great way of seeing the power in these simple questions is to take some real-world examples. Byron Katie has recorded a set of YouTube videos with her taking her guests through each question.

One such example is "my wife wastes her days" [*bit.ly/wastes-days*]. A husband takes issue with the way his wife spends her time with the kids; he feels like he slaves away at work all day, and when he gets back home, he finds that his wife has wasted her day.

Byron: Is it true? Husband: Yes, from my perspective it is.

Byron: Can you absolutely know that it's true? Husband: No.

Byron: How do you react, what happens, when you believe that thought? Husband: I resent her. I feel like I'm working my tail off and I feel like she's a child; I'm picking up after her.

Byron: Who would you be without the thought? Husband: She's beautiful. I'm excited to see her. She's probably been doing cool, creative stuff with our boys. I'd be honoring all the things she does for our world during the day. She does things for us all day.

Byron: So with the thought, you're angry and resentful. Without the thought, you're connected, grateful, appreciative. So how does your wife's day have anything to do with your problem? What you're believing in the moment is the obstacle you're holding between you and your connection with your wife. Beliefs are very powerful. You think the thought, it keeps you blind to your love with her, your connection with her, and everything she does for your two children in your life.

Byron: So that thought, turn that around. Husband: She maximizes her days. I waste my day.

Byron: As far as I'm concerned, a day spent in resentment is a day wasted.

The purpose of The Work

The purpose of The Work is to become curious about all the possibilities of life. We find that this is done most effectively if you remain unattached to any outcome. This is not about valuing one thought above another, but it is about staying truly open to the exploration.

🙏 Gratitude & appreciation

Have you ever saved up for something, bought it, and then felt empty inside? Or perhaps you worked hard to achieve a goal, but realized the journey was more fulfilling than the achievement? This phenomenon is called hedonic adaptation: the idea that people return to a set level of happiness regardless of what happens to them.

In other words, as you earn more, acquire additional things, and achieve higher goals, your expectations also rise in tandem. Ergo, these things result in no permanent gain in happiness. The opposite is also true. When we get used to having less, it takes less to please us.

So naturally, after expecting happiness, but instead feeling emptiness, we start doubting it all. We start focusing on the negative so we continually see the negative. This leads to objectively very successful people being not fully satisfied with their lives.

So are we destined to have feelings of emptiness and inadequacy? It's a fairly depressing prospect, and for many years I was resigned to this case. However, there is a simple tool we found that can transform your outlook: gratitude.

Practicing gratitude

In positive psychology research, gratitude is strongly and consistently associated with greater happiness [*bit.ly/gratitude-allen*]. Gratitude helps people feel more positive emotions, relish good experiences, improve their health, deal with adversity, and build strong relationships.

Practicing it is so simple that it seems there must be a catch. First, you need a prompt to remind you to practice in the morning. We suggest having a Post-it note attached to your bathroom mirror that simply says "gratitude." Every morning when you notice it, repeat the statement "I am grateful for _" five times, and try to keep whatever it is you are grateful for as specific and timely as possible (names of people, specific actions they did, etc.).

For example, "I'm grateful to John for encouraging me when our revenue modeling was inaccurate." Or "I'm grateful to Jane; her help the other day has had such a positive impact on my life."

That's all there is to it! We have seen that a regular practice of gratitude has a marked change on people's outlook, helping them focus on the important things in their life, the things they truly value.

Practicing appreciation

Appreciation is just gratitude stated to the person whom you feel grateful about. It's free to give, yet that simple act can make someone's day, week, or month.

We recommend doing it in writing (text, email, Slack) so that it's easier to give and more impactful when received. In fact, we have a public #shout-out Slack channel that you can give other's appreciation. Just make sure it's specific – appreciating generalities can sometimes come off as insincere.

2. HIRING & ONBOARDING

💎 Hiring 101

Hiring is the most important process in a company. Everything else stems from the ability to hire and retain the right people. In fact, we think that 80% of good management is in making the right hires upfront, and only 20% is in the actual management of those people.

However, if you look across a typical company you'll notice a strange thing: hiring is completely unstandardized. And this is the case not just between teams, but also between candidates! Different candidates interviewing for the same role get evaluated in different ways, and then compared in a most unscientific manner.

This lack of rigor around hiring not only results in bad hires being made, but also in good people being passed over for unsubstantiated reasons. We call this *voodoo hiring*, a term from the book Who: The A Method for Hiring [*bit.ly/smart-a-method*].

> 🗣 "In an age in which every other management process has been studied and codified, we find it amazing that people still view hiring, the process where building an organization begins, as something that resists an orderly approach. Yet managers cling to their favorite methods even when evidence suggests they don't work."
> — *Geoff Smart, Who: The A Method for Hiring*

Voodoo hiring

Imagine trying to submit a scientific paper to a journal describing a trial where you randomized the criteria for every evaluation—you'd be laughed out of the building! You can't measure variables unless you standardize and track them over time.

So why hasn't hiring been standardized? For two reasons:

1. Like the hovering art director [*hoveringartdirectors.tumblr.com*], everyone has their own opinions around hiring. And, more often than not, these opinions are a mixture of subjective principles that are not based in logic.

2. People and departments don't like stepping on each other's toes by pointing out inadequacies in the other's hiring processes.

If you don't give people direction, what do they use to evaluate candidates? Themselves, of course. Ask the average person to describe the ideal hiring process and, more often than not, you'll get a process that spits out a 10/10 score for that person. Everyone likes to hire themselves.

As soon as you start standardizing your hiring process, you will find that critics, fearful of encroachment into their territory, will point out specific inadequacies and use that as evidence that the whole system is a dud.

By all means, listen to them and make any improvements needed. But then point out that an imperfect standardized system is better than no system at all, because the results will be consistent, and therefore can be evaluated against one another. It's important to be quantitative when hiring; it makes the system fairer and helps reduce bias.

Standardized hiring

So what does a standardized hiring system look like? Well, it involves the following things:

- Role proposal focused on outcomes

- Score card used for standardized evaluations

- Standardized screenings

- Standardized interviews: We're going to ask the same questions at the same times in the same order to as many candidates as possible because question consistency enables us to get better insights to more accurately evaluate, compare, and contrast candidates.

- Standardized closing process so that we can iterate on and improve our close rate

It turns out there's an excellent book on this titled Who: The A Method for Hiring [*bit.ly/smart-a-method*], that pioneered the concepts of voodoo hiring and standardized evaluation. It is required reading for any hiring manager at Clearbit (see Recommended reading).

Hiring A players

Hiring also has a huge knock-on effect. You may have heard the Steve Jobs quote:

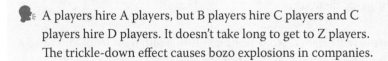 A players hire A players, but B players hire C players and C players hire D players. It doesn't take long to get to Z players. The trickle-down effect causes bozo explosions in companies.

So how exactly do we define an "A player"? Here's the definition we use from Who:

> We define an A player this way: a candidate who has at least a 90 percent chance of achieving a set of outcomes that only the top 10 percent of possible candidates could achieve.

Note: Hiring for A players doesn't mean hiring for the kitchen sink—they can be A players without being talented in every dimension. Talent teams call this looking for "purple squirrels," or perfect candidates who don't actually exist. You need to have a deep understanding of what you need today, and which things can wait until the future.

Consider leverage when adding to your team

Is someone:

* individually so productive that they raise the average productivity of your team?

OR

* acting as a multiplier to everyone else on the team?

If the answer is no to both questions, don't add them to your team. In either case, make sure your overall productivity increase covers the cost of bringing them on.

This prevents leaders from arbitrarily hiring into their team for the sake of building up a fiefdom. Want to add someone? Sure, go ahead, but remember that it raises the bar on expected total per person output.

A picture is worth a thousand words

Throughout this chapter, we reference our golden example: a position we opened for a Head of Revenue Ops. We recommend using the documents we created for that role [*bit.ly/revops-hire*] as a template for your own roles.

Mastering hiring is a superpower

The rest of this chapter will detail how to write a good role proposal; how to source, interview and close incredible candidates; and lastly, how to onboard and align that hire with jobs to be done.

This is a long, multi-year muscle to build, but an incredible superpower once mastered. It's no coincidence that the founders of Benchmark, one of the most successful venture capital firms in all history, were a bunch of recruiters.

✍ Role Proposal

So you want to hire someone? Well, you had better have a good reason for it. You are asking for a $100k–$200k cash investment at the very minimum, not to mention all the hidden costs associated with adding headcount, like ops and communication overhead.

Because of these costs, hiring should be your last resort. At the same time, you need to ensure your team is not understaffed, or else you may find yourself getting pulled into IC work in addition to your managerial and recruiting duties.

Your managerial leverage is your team's output divided by your team's size. In other words, how much are you able to do with as few people as possible? Great managers understand that by hiring the right people you can have a force multiplier effect on the output of your team. And conversely, that by hiring the wrong people (or over-hiring), you reduce your managerial leverage.

A key part of making the right hiring decisions comes from a process of inquiry that helps them justify the hire: a role proposal that explores alternate options, models the ideal candidate, and defines success.

The proposal

As with asking for any investment, you first start out with a proposal—a pitch deck justifying the expense. This should be submitted to both your manager and our People team.

The first failure point of hiring is not being crystal clear about what you really want the person you hire to accomplish. A good proposal will cover that.

 For a good example of a role proposal, see the one we created for our Head of Rev Ops position [*bit.ly/sample-role-proposal*].

External-facing job description

This is a public-facing job description to be posted on our website and on other job sites. This description should include a list of key responsibilities, a list of need-to-haves, and a list of nice-to-haves. This description should take you thirty minutes to one hour to write.

Most companies' job descriptions are relatively boring; don't make that mistake. Write a dynamic and entertaining proposal really selling the company and the position. Remember, you're trying to influence someone to make a fundamental change to their lives, it had better be worth it for them!

Furthermore, A players will already be gainfully employed and performing well. You're pulling them away from comfortable success, so you need to highlight growth opportunities, a culture of success, and the other things that make working here so special.

We recommend including a series of questions at the end of this job description for the candidate to answer when applying. This will let you quickly filter out candidates who are applying to jobs en masse and focus on those who specifically want to work here.

 We recommend using this description for our Rev Ops position as an example [*bit.ly/revops-job-desc*].

Internal facing role scorecard

This should detail how we actually measure what we want this person to accomplish in the first 6–12 months and what attributes they should possess in order to accomplish this. Here is a good example: Scorecard for Head of Revenue Operations [*bit.ly/revops-scorecard*].

From the book *Who*, a scorecard should consist of the following things:

 Mission. Develop a short statement of one to five sentences that describes why a role exists. For example, "The mission for the customer service representative is to help customers resolve their questions and complaints with the highest level of courtesy possible."

Outcomes. Develop three to eight specific, objective outcomes that a person must accomplish to achieve an A performance. For example, "Improve customer satisfaction on a ten-point scale from 7.1 to 9.0 by December 31st."

Competencies. Identify as many role-based competencies as you think appropriate to describe the behaviors someone must demonstrate to achieve the outcomes. Next, identify five to eight competencies that describe your culture, and place those on every scorecard. For example, "Competencies include efficiency, honesty, high standards, and a customer service mentality."

While typical job descriptions break down because they focus on activities, or a list of things a person will be doing (e.g., calling customers, selling), scorecards succeed because they focus on outcomes, or what a person must get done (e.g., grow revenue from $10 million to $15 million in the third quarter).

Level & reporting

We have standardized levels for every role at Clearbit to fairly calculate compensation. Talk to our People team if you're unfamiliar with the different bands.

In this section of your role proposal, also include who the person is reporting to (probably you) and their title.

Salary range

Use our leveling system to find estimated salary ranges.

Metrics to improve

These are metrics that you would expect to improve if we successfully hired for this role.

Alternatives to hiring this person

Give a list of alternatives to hiring this person. This is an important part of the process because it indicates to whoever is approving the role that you have really considered every other option. You might think hiring someone for the position is obvious, but entertain alternatives. Being able to explore the opposite is the mark of an enlightened mind (see Exploring the opposite).

If it's clear you haven't spent much time thinking about alternatives, then prepare for your request to be denied.

What happens if we wait too long to make this hire?

This section should indicate the urgency of the hire. Can we push this hire out for three months, or should we have made it yesterday?

Again, make a real effort to give this an honest answer. A good tactic in startups is to mortgage the future, that is, to punt problems into the future when you will have more time and resources to deal with them. Is this one of those cases?

What next?

Once your proposal is approved, it's time to publish your job description on our site [*bit.ly/revops-scorecard*], and start Sourcing your candidates.

♟ Sourcing

Sourcing good candidates is the hardest part of the recruiting process to make time for, and the easiest part of the process to procrastinate on. It requires a good network, a lot of grunt work sifting through that network, and a lot of rejection. Quite frankly, if you allow it, the process can be really dull.

However, there is no alternative. Clearbit's success hinges on our ability to source great candidates. A good rule of thumb is that every offer requires 10–15 candidates, which requires contacting 100 quality candidates.

When you do not have a lot of quality candidates at the top of the funnel, you compromise further down the funnel. You say to yourself, "while this candidate isn't a great fit, we really need to fill this position," and then you make a bad hire.

But I have other things to do

New managers at Clearbit are sometimes surprised that, after submitting a role proposal, potential candidates don't magically appear waiting to be interviewed. That is not how things work here. You are responsible for sourcing and nurturing your own candidates.

The reason we do this is because it results in higher quality candidates. You are the best person to source candidates because you know better than anyone else exactly what kind of person is needed for the position.

It's also because, given that they will probably work directly for you, you're an integral part of this process. When candidates are evaluating the position, they are just as much evaluating *you* as they are the company.

Diversity

Having a diverse workforce is an important part of building a healthy company. Diversity in background brings diversity of thought, which brings better ideas to the table. Additionally, candidates are increasingly looking at an organization's diversity when evaluating places to work.

In full transparency, we are still figuring out how to do this really well at Clearbit. We recognize that one of our most successful hiring channels (referrals through our network) can also lead to hiring more people from the same background. Improving our overall diversity is one of our 2020 goals.

Ensuring that you have a diverse top-of-funnel (i.e., in the sourcing stage) is an important part of achieving diversity in hiring.

Sourcing tactics

Of all the ways to source candidates, the number one method is via referrals.

Source-a-thons

Source-a-thons are the secret to Clearbit's hiring success. They achieve two things: making sourcing less of a slog, and leveraging the full power of Clearbit's network to find employee referrals.

Clearbit is now at the size that we can source for most roles in our immediate network of employees. Source-a-thons simply gather the most relevant individuals (based on their role and network) in a room for an hour, and dedicate that time to scouring through their networks.

Once you have an approved role proposal in hand, schedule some time with people at the company who have networks related to the role. For example, if you were looking for an engineer, schedule some time with our CTO, Head of Engineering, and a few engineers you know have large networks.

At the start of the meeting, ensure that everyone has read the role proposal. We suggest listing a few sample candidates to help your sourcing group calibrate. Then we're off to the races! Get everyone to scour through their networks (using the tools listed further below), and add the results to a spreadsheet looking like this:

Name	LinkedIn URL	GitHub URL	Email	Can intro?	Notes
James Smith	https://www.linkedin.com/in/jamessmith	github.com/js	james.smith@gmail.com	Yes	Worked with at Thoughtbot; fantastic engineer

For candidates that your sourcing group can intro, ask for an intro right then and there (double-opt-in of course). For the others, either find mutual contacts, or cold-email them after the meeting.

We suggest gamifying the process by giving whoever refers the best candidates a voucher for a fancy dinner. Bringing snacks doesn't hurt either. Speak to our recruiting team to help organize this.

Start by putting together a Google Sheet dedicated to listing candidates for the role. Once the Source-a-thon is over, import this sheet into Lever [lever.co] (our candidate CRM) and put them in a nurture sequence.

Referrals via your own friends and network

When sourcing from your own network, simply sit down and sift through your own Twitter/LinkedIn/Facebook for good candidates. We recommend using one of the tools we list below to do this. Often a quick text or Twitter DM will get a much better response rate than an email.

For those of you who use Twitter, we have seen success by going through your Twitter followers, filtering by role, and then reaching out over Twitter DM. If you have a large Twitter following, tweeting out links to open positions also works.

Sourcing session with new employees

Schedule an hour sourcing session with new employees after they have been at the company for a couple of months. Sit next to them, and comb through their network for open roles. This includes going through their Covey (see the tools list below), their previous colleagues, and whoever they follow on GitHub, Dribble, etc.

We suggest doing prework for this by creating a list of all their old companies, and then pulling up a list of people who work at those companies via Prospector [clearbit.com/prospector]. Then, during the sourcing session, go through the list one by one and ask whether the employee recommends them.

Sourcing session with your ATS

It's also a good idea to source directly from your application tracking system (ATS), in our case Lever. If you have spent time creating a great candidate experience, then you can use your past efforts by reengaging candidates you have already invested time in. It is critical to have detailed reasons for archiving candidates. "Candidate withdrew, not the right time, waiting for promotion."

Use Lever's *snooze* feature to prompt you to follow up with candidates at a later time. Often candidates are interested in a position, but the timing isn't good. Ask them when it would be a good time to re-engage.

Sourcing Session with friends of Clearbit

We have had a lot of success with sitting down with friends who are experts in a field and running a sourcing session with them. Often industry experts will have a good idea of up-and-comers in their field.

Once you have a list of candidates, get a warm intro through that friend; their introduction will carry some social proof.

Customers

Note down particularly interesting interactions with customers who are clearly very sharp—they may turn out to be great candidates. They already know you and the company, which is a huge shortcut.

You can search our internal customer database for people (via SQL on our Analytics DB) whose roles and seniority matches your requirements and start there.

AngelList & AList (engineer-specific)

AngelList and AList are both tools you can use to drum up some engineering candidates, although often of varying quality. AngelList is inbound and AList outbound. We recommend starting with AList.

The key to using these tools is to do some aggressive filtering to limit yourself to a manageable number of candidates. For example, exclude engineers without an avatar, a GitHub account, or a personal website and blog. In the engineering world, the latter represents a good signal. Writing about your craft is a good indication that you have passion for it.

Then send a customized, targeted message to a candidate. For example, compliment them on a particularly interesting GitHub repo they worked on.

Outbound

Outbound is the most grueling way to source, but it can work. Again, the key is aggressive filtering and customized messages.

Make a list of companies who are well known for hiring great people in the role you're trying to fill. Go through Prospector [*clearbit.com/prospector*] or LinkedIn Recruiter to find a list of their employees.

We suggest keeping the message short and simple, and then link to some "fun Clearbit facts" [*bit.ly/cb-fun-facts*]. Another approach is to write up a fun description [*bit.ly/clearbit-x*] of the team, the role, and the company.

Lead with a standout subject line that will make candidates want to open the email. "Hello" works surprisingly well, or "I would love to work with you." Additionally, emails that end with "Thanks in advance" get a better response rate.

As a hiring manager, you can also leverage your CEO and executive team for outbound! A short note from the CEO will often get a more positive response than one from your recruiting team. Using Lever, you can send nurture sequences from whomever you'd like without bothering them.

Aline Lerner, founder of interviewing.io, has a great presentation on sourcing [*bit.ly/sourcing-for-founders*] that she gives to founders. She says:

 "It's hard to get enough info about people to write great personalized messages, but when it's possible, it's SO much better. I'd even venture to say that for every 100 impersonal, automated messages you send (unless you're a household name like Google), you're better off spending like 30 minutes stalking someone and writing something about how their past work resonates with what you're doing."
— *Aline Lerner, interviewing.io*

Ask for feedback

Following the *if you want money, ask for feedback* model, this technique involves asking the people you might want to hire for feedback on your job description.

Once you've written a compelling job description and gotten some real feedback from your team, create a simple email like this:

Hi Erin!

Your name came up when I was chatting with Ashley Taylor, and she mentioned that you were an incredibly talented Product Marketer and someone she looked up to while at Yext.

I'm starting to build out our PMM team here at Clearbit, and I'd love to chat for a few minutes if you're willing.

Mostly I would love advice on how to think about the first 2–4 PMM hires and how you would structure that org if you were starting over.
Would also really appreciate any feedback you have for me on the early job description <insert link> I've put together.

Let me know if you'd be willing to grab a quick call sometime next week!

Remember, if they're not interested, it's possible that they know of other good candidates. Ask them.

Recruiters

Recruiters should often be the last resort, since the pool of candidates they send through typically aren't of the same quality as you'd find when sourcing through your own network. However, recruiters excel at filling certain types of roles such as go-to-market roles (e.g., CSMs), since these are evergreen roles with typically a high volume of candidates.

We have also found a difference between recruiting companies and recruiting freelancers in that the latter tend to bring in higher quality candidates.

Tools

Name	Description	Temperature	Site
Vettery	Job marketplace	warm	vettery.com
Teamable	Search your network	cold	teamable.com
Covey	Search your network	cold	getcovey.com

Name	Description	Temperature	Site
AngelList	Job postings & candidates	warm	angel.co
AList	List of vetted candidates	warm	alist.co
Underdog	Job marketplace	warm	underdog.io
LinkedIn Recruiter	Search for candidates	cold	linkedin.com
Interviewing.io	Pre-vetted engineers	cold	Interviewing.io

 Interviewing

The basics

So you've got your proposal approved and you've screened some candidates who are interested; you're making progress—great work! The next step is interviewing and evaluating candidates. The good news is that this is easier than Sourcing because it's a process that's entirely within your control.

As we explained in Hiring 101, we have a standardized interview process at Clearbit to ensure consistency and rigor.

The five types of interviews are:

1. Screening Interviews

2. Top-grading interviews

3. Focused Interviews

4. Values interviews

5. Reference interviews

Every candidate goes through all five types. Focused interviews and values interviews are best done in person onsite, and preferably back-to-back on the same day. The others (Screening, Top-grading) can be done prior to the onsite interview via Zoom/phone calls (to save time).

Our recruiting team will coordinate the day onsite, but it is your responsibility to determine who's going to interview the candidate and the different areas they should each cover. It's a waste of time (and boring for the candidate) if there's too much overlap in questions.

Fairly often, candidates won't be able to dedicate a full day onsite for interviews. In these cases, we'll split out interviews over two days.

Sample interview schedule

Time	Activity
09:00	Candidate arrives and is greeted by the hiring manager (you) and a member of our recruiting team.
9:00 – 11:00am	Focussed interviews
11:00am – 12:00pm	Culture interview
12:00pm – 12:45pm	Lunch with hiring manager
1:00pm – 4:00pm	Focused interviews
16:00	Recruiter thanks the candidate and explains next steps
4:15pm (or immediately next day)	Huddle to determine a yes/no decision to move forward and conduct reference calls

🫤 Screening Interviews

The screening interview is a short phone call designed to weed out candidates quickly. Since interviews are incredibly expensive in terms of opportunity cost, we want to ensure that time is only spent on A players.

As with all our interviews, we run screen checks in a structured manner to ensure consistency and rigor.

Four essential questions

We recommend scheduling the screening call for 30 minutes.

Open the call by setting the context: *"I'm really looking forward to our time together. Here's what I'd like to do. I'd like to spend the first twenty minutes of our call getting to know you. You may hear me making some notes. After that, I'm happy to answer any questions you may have so you can get to know us. Sound good?"*

Most candidates who are interested in the job will happily agree. Then, progress with the following four questions, writing notes along the way.

What are your career goals? Here we are trying to determine whether there is intention to a candidate's career, or if it's an aimless wandering. The best candidates know what they want to do and speak with passion and energy; filter all others out.

What are you really good at professionally? Please give me some examples. Here we are trying to determine 5–10 areas that the candidate considers themselves really good at. Don't accept one-word answers; press for examples. If these strengths don't align with the scorecard, filter the candidate out.

What is your greatest accomplishment professionally? What are you most proud of? This should be a shining example of what the candidate is capable of, one that is backed by real numbers. You may find that you don't need to use this question if it's already clear what the candidate's strengths are.

What are you not good at or not interested in? Please give me some examples. This is better than asking "what are your weaknesses," as it often yields more insightful responses. If you're getting cookie-cutter responses, say, "That sounds like a strength to me. What are you really not good at or not interested in doing?"

This question is often hard for folks. One tactic is to wait until they've given some answers and then say, *"Well, what if we asked your current boss? What would they say you're not good at or not interested in?"*

Once you have an answer to that, ask about their peers' feedback: *"Well, what if we asked your team? What would they say you're not good at or not interested in?"*

 "I sometimes ask this question by qualifying it with, 'We all have parts of the job that we don't love, that don't give us energy, and we find ourselves procrastinating to complete. For me, I don't love X, so I wait for the end of the day to do it. What would you say is that part of the job that you don't love, but you know you have to do?' This approach might be a little too soft, but I always get honest answers."
— *Brianna Byun, Recruiting at Clearbit*

Who were your last three managers, and how will they each rate your performance on a scale of 1–10 when we talk with them? Why?

Notice we say *when* rather than *if;* we are trying to provoke some honesty. Get full names of the managers, not titles. Ask the candidate to spell their full names clearly for you. This sends the message you're recording this information to use it later. When a candidate is uncomfortable with a manager or situation, they will call it out specifically, which is helpful.

Lots of 8/9/10 is good. 7 is neutral. 1–6 is bad. If there are too many 6s, screen out. But listen carefully—the best candidates may be diamonds in the rough.

Getting curious to know more

Rather than trying to come up with clever questions, there is a much easier way of teasing the information you need out of candidates. Simply prompt them to continue down their train of thought. You can accomplish this by saying, "oh? tell me more," or by repeating the last few words they've said.

Selling

If by twenty minutes in you think they are an A player, move into sell mode. Interviews are a big commitment for candidates, and the best candidates will be getting hounded by other companies, so they need to know it's worth their time.

First, ask if it's possible to extend the call by 15 minutes. Then start pitching.

Selling works best when you let them ask questions. Rather than telling them how great we are, let them ask you questions, which gives you more info on what they care about and then allows you to tailor your selling answers to the questions they are asking.

We recommend you start by saying something like "okay, so you've been under the microscope a bit and now it's my turn. I'm happy to talk about whatever is helpful. What can I tell you about Clearbit, the team, myself, or the role?"

The pitch

Different candidates require different pitches. Ideally, the first part of the interview should give you an indication of where to focus your efforts.

Ask them what they're interested in next. Are they interested in smaller companies? Focus on our values of autonomy and iteration speed. Are they interested in a big win on their CV? Focus on our progress to date and ambitions. Are they going to be remote? Focus on how flexible our remote culture is.

If they're going to be reporting to you, speak to yourself and the rest of the team you've built. Talk about how much we value management at Clearbit, and the attributes of great management that are important to you.

Ask the candidate questions to learn about their lives and what they want to optimize for next. Is it great management, an inspiring mission, or financial compensation? It's important to note these down in Lever, because this information will be useful during the Closing process.

Make sure to leave time for them to ask you questions. They are interviewing us as well.

At the end of the phone interview, let the candidate know that you would like to immediately schedule the next interview (which is usually a remote top-grading interview). We suggest giving a brief overview of our interview process so they know what to expect (our recruiting team will reiterate this too).

🎩 Top-grading interviews

The goal of this interview is to understand the candidate's story and patterns. These stories and patterns are predictive of the candidate's future performance.

With a top-grading interview, you are working through the candidate's last five positions (in chronological order), asking a set of questions to determine how successful they were. It's important that the hiring manager responsible for the role is the one who conducts this interview.

Our top-grading interview is inspired by the Who interview in Who: The A Method for Hiring [*bit.ly/smart-a-method*]. This style of interviewing is the most valid and reliable predictor of performance, according to a half-century's worth of thousands of research studies in the field of industrial psychology.

Opening the interview

It can be an intense interview, so open it by preparing the candidate for what's ahead:

"Thank you for taking the time to visit with us today. As we have already discussed, we are going to do a chronological interview to walk through each job you have held. For each job, I am going to ask you five core questions: What were you hired to do? What accomplishments are you most proud of? What were some low points during that job? Who were the people you worked with? Why did you leave that job?

"I'll be making notes live throughout the interview. At the end of the interview, you will have a chance to ask me questions.

"Finally, while this sounds like a lengthy interview, it will go remarkably fast. I want to make sure you have the opportunity to share your full story, so it is my job to guide the pace of discussion. Sometimes, we'll go into more depth into a period of your career. Other times, I will ask that we move on to the next topic. I'll try to make sure we leave plenty of time to cover your most recent and, frankly, most relevant jobs.

"Does that make sense?"

Top-grading questions

The questions are as follows. Make notes throughout the interview, because you will not remember enough afterward. You should ask these questions for each job the candidate has held over the last five years, starting at their earliest job.

What were you hired to do? Here you are trying to discover the scorecard for the candidate's job, had they written one. What were the missions and key outcomes? What competencies might have mattered? A players should know this like the back of their hand.

What were your priorities? What did you accomplish, and how? A players talk about outcomes linked to expectations; they talk about concrete results. B and C players talk about events and people; aspects but not results. Ideally these accomplishments should match up with the position's scorecard.

What were some low points during that job? These can be difficult to tease out of candidates, but don't stop until you have something of substance. Keep reframing the question; for example, "What was your biggest mistake?" "What was your biggest lesson learned?" "What would you have done differently?"

Who was on your team? How were those relationships? You want a list of names you can potentially reference check, particularly if the relationship wasn't good.

What was your primary manager's name? Ask for the spelling because it shows the candidate that you're going to reference check them directly, and thus inspires honesty in the next question.

How did your manager rate your performance on a scale of one to ten? Asking for a score will help make the answer more concrete. Once you have a score, ask the candidate to elaborate. For example, what strengths will your manager mention? What weaknesses?

What were your reasons for leaving? This final question will give you an insight into what motives the candidate and how they think about their career. Was the candidate promoted, recruited, or fired from each job along their career progression? Keep digging; don't accept vague answers.

Master tactics

- Use the candidate's answers as a tool to dig in more by asking "What," "How," and "Tell me more" questions.

- You have to interrupt the candidate. It's more rude to let them ramble or waste time. Show enthusiasm about the story they are telling and guide them back online with a targeted question.

- Consider their accomplishments and outcomes in context with the three Ps. Compare to *previous*? Compare to *plan*? Compare to *peers*?

- Put yourself in their shoes—get specific information rather than general. Facts are king!

- Look for stop signs (inconsistencies in body or language) and dig in and ask for more info.

🔬 Focused Interviews

This is the part of the interview that will differ depending on what kind of role you're hiring for. For engineers, you may want to do a pair-programming session; for sales, you might want a mock sales call. It should cover what their work will look like day-to-day (i.e., no writing code on whiteboards).

The golden rule is to ensure that these focused interviews are *standardized*; each candidate for the role should be asked the same questions. Otherwise, how are you to evaluate them against one another?

Make sure these interviews are focused on the outcomes and competencies of the scorecard, not some vaguely defined job description or manager's intuition. Leave 10 minutes at the end for questions (and make sure any questions asked are included with the rest of the interview feedback—they're a valuable insight into what the candidate cares about).

Every department has a page in the wiki indicating how they do their focused interviews. For example, here's what a technical interview might look like. Each topic has standardized questions, which are detailed in our wiki.

Aline Lerner, founder of interviewing.io, has written a good piece on the type of questions [*bit.ly/best-interviewers*] she recommends asking during technical interviews.

 "Recruiting isn't about vetting as much as it is about selling... being a good interviewer takes time and effort and a fundamental willingness to get out of autopilot and engage meaningfully with the other person."

– Aline Lerner in What do the best interviewers have in common? [*bit.ly/best-interviewers*]

Focused interview topic	Time	Notes
Product / Process	30 minutes	Run by someone on our product team.
Pair programming	2 hours	This is either backend or frontend focused.
Algorithm / System Design	30-60 mins	Run by a senior engineer

Splitting up responsibilities

Take the scorecard and group the outcomes and responsibilities it lists. Then divvy up each group to your interviewers, ensuring that they're all covered. You want to avoid having different interviewers asking the same questions to the candidate; it's both a waste of time and boring to the candidate.

Example from *Who*

Who has a good example of how to run a focused sales interview, reprinted below:

> For example, let's say you are hiring a VP of sales. The scorecard you created has four outcomes on it:
>
> 1. Grow domestic sales from $500 million to $600 million by December 31, and continue growing them by 20 percent per year for the next five years.
> 2. Maintain at least a 45 percent gross margin across the portfolio of products annually.
> 3. "Who" the sales organization, ensuring that 90 percent or more of all new hires are A Players as defined by the sales scorecards. Achieve a 90 percent or better ratio of A Players across the team within three years through hiring and coaching. Remove all chronic C Players within ninety days of identification.
> 4. Create a sales strategy that the CEO approves during the annual planning cycle.
>
> In addition, let's say you have identified six competencies that define success in the job:
>
> 1. Aggressive
> 2. Persistent
> 3. Hires A Players

4. Holds people accountable
5. Follows through on commitments
6. Open to criticism and feedback

Try assigning three members of your team to perform focused interviews based on this scorecard. The first interviewer takes the first two outcomes and the first two competencies because they all have to do with growing sales and managing costs and the behaviors that support both. The second interviewer has the responsibility for the outcome related to Who and the two competencies having to do with how the candidate builds the team. That leaves everything else for the third interviewer.

Each interview should take forty-five minutes to one hour, depending on how many outcomes and competencies you assign to each interviewer. Regardless of the time spent, each interviewer will bring supplemental data to your decision-making process.

Values interviews

At Clearbit, we place a particular emphasis on building a close-knit team. We want to work with people whom we also enjoy spending time with. It's one of the things that makes this place so fun. Therefore, we look to hire people who are aligned with our core values and will add to the culture we've created. The Values interview is designed to determine this.

Using Clearbit's hiring rubric

Our hiring rubric is a tool designed to assist hiring managers and interviewers with making better hiring decisions. It determines the character traits we think our candidates need in order to be successful within Clearbit's culture.

By externalizing the subjective portion of the hiring process that often takes place in our heads, we can be more objective and scale our character evaluation abilities. Below are our values; each candidate gets a score of zero to four by each value.

Trait	Description
Self sufficient	Candidate is a self-starter, and once given a general direction or problem-set they will run with it.
Trust	Candidate only has to be told something once, and you can be confident it will get done.
Conviction	Candidate is willing to disagree (playfully) and fight for what they believe in.
Loves their craft	Candidate has genuine curiosity and love for their craft – it's not just another job for them.
Integrity	Candidate is honest and truthful.
Sense of humour	Candidate is quick to laugh and doesn't take themselves or life too seriously.
Team	Candidate works well with others and believes there's no such thing as "it's not my job."

Now, you may be thinking that testing for these values could be quite arbitrary. You would be right, were it not for our hiring rubric, which details how to test against each value.

Our full rubric can be found in the wiki under the *Recruiting* section, but we've reprinted a portion of it below as an example:

Sample rubric: testing for craft

At Clearbit, we take pride in what we do, and we're always looking for ways that we can improve. Mastering our craft and bettering ourselves should be an end unto itself. We want to add people to the team who take a similar joy in their work.

Some ideas for testing:

- Does the candidate have a blog (doesn't need to be up to date)?

- Has the candidate published any works, written any books, or given any presentations?

- Does the candidate know any experts in their field well?

- Has the candidate shown clear progression in their field over the last few years?

- Is the candidate aware of recent news/research/articles that you haven't even heard of?

- Does the candidate have any side hobbies related to the field?

- Has the candidate purposely chosen this career or just slipped into it?

- Do other people/companies seek their advice?

- If they're an engineer, do they develop or maintain any open source projects?

- Are they part of the community for their specialty; e.g., do they attend meetups, conferences, etc.?

How to score

- A **zero** would be someone whose knowledge has remained static for the last few years, takes no pleasure in their work, and clocks out at 5 p.m.

- A **four** would be someone who's taught themselves their field from scratch, is constantly reading and looking to improve, and has lots of coffees with people looking for their advice.

📞 Reference interviews

Reference interviews are to double-check the accuracy of what candidates have told us, to uncover any issues before we potentially make a bad hire, to address any red/yellow flags that were raised during the interview process, and lastly to help the hiring manager best work with the candidate once we've hired them.

There are two types of reference interviews:

1. *Direct references* – interviews with people that the candidate has directly referred to us.

2. *Indirect references* – interviews with people that the candidate hasn't referred to us. These people are found through our network, cold emailing, etc.

You should try and do at least three of each.

Direct references

These are still useful to do, but know that 99% of the time direct references offered unprompted by the candidate will be positively glowing. Why else would the candidate have referred you to these people if otherwise? So you have to become an expert in teasing out the real juicy details.

Listen for red flags like hesitations and intentional omissions. Ask for facts and not anecdotes. Exactly which parts of their team's success were they responsible for?

Picking the references based on screening and top-grading (e.g., their last five managers), you will usually get less gushy answers. However, sometimes this just isn't possible for all the references you'd like; for example, if they're still working at another company.

The script

Ask for a twenty-minute reference call (preferably a video call over Zoom). As with every part of our interview process, the process is standardized. Here's the script we use:

In what context did you work with the person? Discount references who only know the candidate's work by hearsay.

What were the person's biggest strengths?

What were the person's biggest areas for improvement back then? It is very important to say "back then." This liberates people to talk about real weaknesses, assuming that the candidate has improved them by now. (In reality, past performance is an indicator of future performance.)

How would you rate his/her overall performance in that job on a scale of 1-10? What about his/her performance causes you to give that rating? A concrete score forces people to think objectively and compare that person's performance to that of the rest of the team.

The person mentioned that he/she struggled with ____ in that job. Can you please tell me more about that? This is a good chance to dig into any issues that might have been raised during the interview process.

Tell me about a time that you and ___ disagreed. How did you resolve that disagreement? This is a good way of digging into how the candidate deals with conflict.

Would you hire him/her again if you could?

Indirect references

If the candidate is still gainfully employed, then these have to be *very* carefully done, but indirect references are usually where you get the most candid feedback. Try to find people that the candidate has directly worked with in the past, either directly or indirectly, and get them on the phone.

Use the company's resources to find appropriate candidates. Ask in Slack whether anyone has any contacts at the candidate's previous workplaces. Lastly, look on LinkedIn to find appropriate people. Use Connect [*connect.clearbit.com*] to find their email addresses if necessary.

Once you have them on the phone, follow the script above.

ᛜ Closing

Time spent closing candidates is arguably your most leveraged time spent compared to anything else you could be doing. The old adage "do things that don't scale" applies here; you're dealing with so few candidates that you can do unique and extraordinary things to help increase the chance they accept. Because of this leverage, don't shy away from asking senior people (including our CEO) to help close.

The other adage to bear in mind is "time kills all deals." We can win offers just by moving faster than the next company.

 Most of this section on closing was written by Eric Feldman [*twitter.com/ericmfeldman*] with additions from Matthew Strassberg [*skyrocketventures.com*].

Selling

Prior to closing the candidate, you want to get them as excited as possible about Clearbit. In fact, you should be selling at every touchpoint throughout the interview process. On the first call, you should establish the candidate's motivations, and then throughout the process be able to reframe the opportunity to align with the candidate's needs. If you wait to start selling the role at the end of the process, you will probably lose the candidate.

Put yourself in their shoes. Ask the candidate questions to learn about their lives and what they want to optimize for. Is it great management, an inspiring mission, or financial compensation? Hopefully you will have done the groundwork here on the screening call, so you can look at your notes.

We find the typical motivators are cash compensation, scope of role, company growth, culture, location, and industry. You should frame the company's value in a way that's aligned with each candidate's core motivations.

Your pitch per candidate will vary, but here are some of the things we suggest:

The five 'fs'

* Fit (talents and strengths match to opportunity and role)

* Family support for joining company

* Freedom to make decisions

* Fortune and glory

* Fun

The opportunity

- Scope the opportunity—don't be afraid to help candidates do the math.

- If you're interested in working closely with the leadership team, you may be especially suited to Clearbit.

- Share the product roadmap.

- Talk about the other people on the team and their caliber.

- Talk about Clearbit's potential, our latest funding raise, and our ambitions.

- Talk about career progression and the things candidates could learn (and what we can learn from them in return).

Self growth and values

Show how seriously we take self-growth and our values.

- Internally we have an incredible culture of feedback and self-growth. Conscious Leadership [*blog.alexmaccaw.com/conscious-leadership*] and world-class management are at the heart of everything we do, and it shows. We score an average of 8.5 out of 10 when we anonymously survey our employees' happiness, and we have only 5% annual employee attrition.

- Send this blog post [*clearbit.com/blog/remote-work-growth*].

- And these:

  » "Feedback is not a dirty word" [*bit.ly/maccaw-feedback*]

  » "Managers Handbook TLDR" [*clearbit.com/blog/managers-handbook-tldr*]

Talk benefits

* Talk about the amount of fun we have at Clearbit (send pictures of our offsites).

* Therapy via Modern Health

* Education stipend

* If the candidate is in SF, make sure to have them in for lunch.

Provide social proof

* Encourage the candidate to do reference checks.

* For senior candidates, offer to connect them with our investors.

* Send them and their significant other flowers and/or champagne.

* Ask mutual friends to reach out and provide positive references of the company.

Pre-close

Prior to closing the candidate, use this template to prepare the candidate and gather the necessary information to put together an offer. It's important that **at no stage** do we indicate for certain that they are getting an offer.

State excitement and hint offer is coming soon: *"We're conducting final references, doing a final team sync, but we're extremely excited about you. Just wanted to take a second to sync here on some final items."*

Pre-close statement: *"Assuming we extended an offer to you that made sense financially, do you see yourself joining Clearbit?"*

Potential answer one: candidate says "Yes"

If they did not hesitate, and Clearbit is the first choice, ask these additional questions:

1. *"Have you discussed Clearbit with your significant other or anyone else required to make a decision?"*

2. *"Theoretically, if everything were to work out, when is the earliest you could start?"*

Potential answer two: candidate is unsure whether or not they'd join

1. Ask very candidly:

    1. *"What questions do you have with Clearbit?"*

    2. *"What other options are you considering?"*

2. Ask candidates to complete the sentence: *"I would join the company as long as ___"*; they will tell you what is in the way of them joining. Often you'll be surprised at how easy it can be to address their questions.

3. Repeat back what they said:

    1. *"What I heard is___. If those conditions were met theoretically, would you see yourself joining Clearbit?"*

    2. Take notes on this and send in a comprehensive email follow-up to the candidate to demonstrate commitment to them.

4. Ask *"What is your timeline for making a decision?"*

Potential answer three: Candidate insists that they just want an offer first and then will consider things after

1. The likelihood of them joining is lower, but you just ultimately have to go ahead. Agree with that idea cheerily: *"Absolutely! We're super stoked and will be getting back to you ASAP."*

2. Ask, *"What is your timeline for making a decision?"*

3. End with:

   1. *"Great, well, we should be finishing up soon here and we'll get back to you very quickly. As mentioned, the team is pretty stoked. Talk soon."*

   2. Follow up this conversation with an email reiterating your understanding of what they've said. This builds trust and gives them the confidence that they are being heard (e.g., *"What I heard is__"*).

Before an offer: do's and don'ts

Do not: Lead the candidate to believe that they can get any added benefits/perks beyond your intended offer unless you are sure they can (e.g., raises, annual refreshes).

Do: Tell them "yes" or "no" only if you are 100% sure. If you are not sure if you are willing/able to give them what they are suggesting, just say something like *"I don't know about that; that's not typical. I'll look into it, but let's assume the answer is no for now."*

Do not: Tell them you will make an offer as soon as you determine they're qualified for your company. Until reaching that point, do not say or indicate that you will definitely make an offer. After all, you may not.

Do: Say *"we like you,"* or *"it would be great to have you on our team,"* etc. Tell them you are very interested, would love to have them aboard, and will be discussing/deliberating/deciding on a compensation package, and that you *"hope to reach an agreement with them."*

Do not: Tell them when to expect to receive an offer from you.

Do: Tell them it's up to them; that you only want to make an offer **if you have reached mutual agreement on terms.** Candidates are understandably eager to get to the finish line asap, and would love to collect an offer from you asap. But you should only make the offer when the candidate is ready to accept it. You should work with the candidate to get to that point asap.

Do not: Tell them how much time they can have or that they can have time, or refer to any deadline.

Do: Remind them that interviews are ongoing and that you will consider hiring any of those people until the position is filled, so if the candidate does decide they want to work at your company, it will help if they can figure that out as soon as possible. After all, waiting too long may result in the position being filled by someone else instead.

Do not: Discuss any compensation we are thinking of giving them—salary, equity, or otherwise—prior to the offer call.

Do: Tell them about the past, present, and potential future valuation of the company. Give them hypotheticals rather than promises of what will happen in the future. If you do want to talk about the incremental value of an amount of stock that would approximate their offer, then manage their expectations by discussing the value of an amount that is the same or a little lower than what you intend to offer. For example, if you plan on offering .2%, tell them how much .1% is worth. Certainly don't discuss what .5% or 1% is worth if you plan on offering .2%, as you might inflate the candidate's expectations beyond what they will get in their package. Sell them even more thoroughly on the things that are not tied to how much you decide to offer them, such as benefits, the job itself, growth opportunities, technology, etc.

Do not: Ask the candidate to email you, or email the candidate anything that desires a response. Your talks with the candidate should only be live (on the phone or in person). Emails can delay communication (and in some cases are not received at all!), they obscure or distort communication, and they are also often used by candidates to create distance. For example, when candidates decide to withdraw from consideration by your company, they almost always decide to do so through email, so that they can avoid confrontation and the possibility of being persuaded otherwise. All of those problematic scenarios caused by using email for communication are the opposite of what you want.

Do: Coordinate your communication with your recruiter. If urgent, then call the candidate rather than emailing them.

Do not: Tell the candidate or give them any indication that they are your top choice, or that you don't have any other candidates. Even if that is indeed true at the moment, it may soon change, as you should keep pursuing/interviewing candidates until there is no longer an opening. Also, you don't want to give the candidate a false sense of entitlement.

Do: Tell the candidate that you like them a lot, you think they're great, etc. Tell them the reasons you like them. People like hearing why others like them, and they tend to reciprocate that liking. One suggestion is to read out positive feedback that the team gave the candidate during the interview process.

Offer and closing

Typically, there are three different methods of making offers to candidates:

1. Make the offer with no deadline.

2. Make the offer with an immediate deadline (a.k.a. the "exploding offer" or "hard close")

3. Don't make the offer unless it will be accepted (a.k.a. **"Don't make an offer! Reach an agreement!"**)

We recommend the third method for the following reasons:

- We have a standardized leveling system for compensation that ensures that offers are fair; we do not want it to seem like the door is open for negotiation.

- The candidate won't ever be in limbo, mulling over whether or not to accept your offer.

- The candidate won't be able to shop your offer around.

While rare, there may be circumstances where it is best to deviate from this and choose the first or the second method. This is usually when you need to apply some time pressure when there are multiple candidates to choose between.

Make the offer

As with a marriage proposal, the key is not to make the offer until you're sure they're going to accept!

Explain the package

Remind candidates about the work we are doing with our Compensation Consultants to come up with our ranges.

"We worked with a compensation consultant to develop a system of career levels and associated salary ranges. This new system is helping to make offers competitive by paying market. It also allows us to create a much more fair system for existing and future employees by removing negotiation from the picture; otherwise, we just reward great negotiators rather than basing offers on the market."

Remember, this system is designed so we pay in the top percentile of the market, rather than just market.

Reach an agreement

Ask them, *"If we were to make you the following offer* (state the offer in full detail, including cash, equity, benefits, etc), *would you accept?"*

Make the offer

If they say yes, then make the offer. If you skip this step and simply make them the offer, then it is very common for them to ask for a few more things after the fact (e.g., signing bonus, moving expenses, etc). You will then be in the awkward position of having to give these (but then a political culture begins) or starting the relationship on a negative note by saying no.

It is better to get the candidate to pre-agree in full detail before making the offer. Then the relationship begins with a resoundingly positive *"Yes! Thank you! I'm so excited!"*

You should have covered benefits by this point, but if the candidate has any questions, reiterate the benefits and send over the PDF where they're all covered.

Telling the Equity Story

Some candidates are coming from more established companies where their base salary is much higher. Other candidates lack a deeper understanding of the value of equity and don't prioritize it when evaluating offers. In these cases, it's important to not just give offer details, but to tell a story about the potential value the offer represents.

1. Make a copy of our equity calculator (ask the People team).

2. Fill in salary and shares with the candidate's offer.

3. Explain that we review salary and equity and you can expect to get grants if you're performing well.

4. Discuss best and worst case scenarios – what their equity could be worth in 2–10 years.

5. Share An Engineer's Guide to Stock Options [*bit.ly/maccaw-stock*] (relevant to not just engineers), and our public commitment [*clearbit.com/blog/stock*] to ensure that everyone can exercise them.

Delivering the offer: do's and don'ts

Do not: Make more than one offer. Do not tell a candidate there is wiggle room in your offer or that it is negotiable, or that they can have more time to think about it. The exception is if you are making someone an offer with several options of base salary and equity combinations. Do not increase your offer if a candidate who has said they would accept your offer asks for you to increase it from what they already said they would accept!

Do: When you make the offer, you should expect that they will immediately verbally accept it. That is what they should have said they would do at this point, and you should hold them accountable to their word. So if the person responds to your offer with *"I'll think about it"* or anything other than *"I accept,"* then respond by saying something like *"our understanding was that you would definitely accept an offer at this level."*

Sending the offer letter

Remember that an offer letter is a formality and is "the fine print" following the candidate's verbal acceptance of your offer. It should not be a time for the candidate to negotiate further. You should, of course, answer any questions that arise, but as long as your offer letter language is fairly standard, with no unusual terms or surprises, then the candidate should agree to it, sign it, and return it quickly.

Post close

Too many candidates are lost because they feel abandoned once they are given an offer or arrive at the company. Think lots of touches!

Send them a congratulatory email and follow up with flowers and/or champagne to them (and their SO). Our recruiting team will coordinate with you to send an email to them and CC the entire company, so everyone can chime in on how excited they are about your candidate joining.

Legal

Clearbit is an equal opportunity employer. We value and celebrate how you identify, who you love, the color of your skin, your age (at heart and on paper), the gods you do or don't believe in, and every other belief and characteristic that make you YOU. The more inclusive we are, the better we—and our work—will be.

 Onboarding

So you've successfully interviewed and hired a candidate. Congratulations—nice work! However, before you get too carried away, there's one last step: onboarding.

If hires are not onboarded properly, then one of two things will happen: they will quit within the first six months or, even worse, they will be ineffective.

A successful onboarding process achieves these things:

* Reassures the hire that they've made the right decision

* Introduces the hire to key stakeholders

- Gives the hire the tools they need to do their job (e.g., a set-up laptop, access to GitHub)

- Gives the hire context around the history of the company, product line, culture, etc.

- Sets up the hire's first 90 days, decides on key metrics

- Lets them hit the ground running

Location

Nothing beats in-person time for bonding, trust building, and quick communication, so we fly people out to Clearbit headquarters in San Francisco for their first two weeks whenever possible.

The 30/60/90 plan

A 30/60/90 is simply a plan of what hires will do in their first 90 days. Ideally it should closely align with the Role Proposal you created for the job in the first place.

A good 30/60/90 will be:

- Very specific, with goals orientated around the original role proposal.

- Quantifiable, with specific targets to hit.

- Bought into. Ideally the hire, having seen the role proposal, is going to come up with their own 30/60/90 that you will sign off on. This will ensure that they have bought into the plan.

- Achievable. Hires should be getting easy wins early on.

We suggest splitting out things the hire should learn from things the hire should do, as well as splitting things out by time period.

We have created a sample 30/60/90 [*bit.ly/sample-306090*] for you to use as inspiration. Here's an excerpt:

📖 **Day 1-30**

> Goal: Meet everyone, gain context, figure out how to find answers for different foundational questions, and then find them.
>
> Learn:
>
> • What do the products do?
>
> • Who are the types of people who use them? Why?
>
> • What do all the teams do? What are their goals and targets?
>
> • What does the growth team do? How does the team work together?
>
> • What content exists? What's the content creation and publishing process?
>
> • What data is available? Where does it come from?
>
> Do:
>
> • Participate in ongoing content projects: data playbook, CMO book, persona pages, etc.
>
> • Demonstrate knowledge around SQL joins (e.g., the difference between OUTER and INNER)

- Create drip campaign for leads awaiting response

- Create re-engagement campaign for signup flow abandonment

- Publish a blog post

Clearbit Academy

Early in our history, our leadership team used to do one-on-ones with every new hire. These were an important aspect of onboarding new people and relationship building.

As the company grew, it became untenable to meet everyone individually, so we batch up these meetings into something we call Clearbit Academy, which we run on the last Friday of every month.

Clearbit Academy is about giving new hires (and existing employees) a clearer sense of who we are, what is important to us, and how to be successful in their new roles. Throughout the day, every team presents an overview. This includes team history, key people, how the team is structured, and how best to work with the team.

Check out our wiki for more information on Clearbit Academy and recordings of previous sessions.

Schedule

Day zero

Before the hire's official start date, we send them the 15 Commitments of Conscious Leadership [*bit.Ly/15-commitments*]. Our Ops team will also collect a brief bio and send a mass email to the entire team, introducing them to the new hire.

Day one

A new hire's first day is all about getting set up, starting to bond with their teammates, and having their first one-one-one.

By day two, we want new hires to feel like they know where to find things, who to ask for help, and how they'll be working with their manager.

Suggested first day schedule

1. Tech and HR onboarding *

2. Assigned the general onboarding project [bit.ly/onboard-sample] in Asana *

3. Added to your team-specific onboarding project [bit.ly/onboard-team-sample] in Asana

4. Assigned an onboarding buddy who is their go-to for questions during their first two weeks

5. Welcome meeting scheduled with their team

6. First one-on-one with their manager

Ops team will coordinate

First week

Week one is about learning, gathering context, meeting with teammates, and writing a 30/60/90-day plan. They should be going through the Asana checklist, reading the linked materials, and checking off the tasks.

By the end of week one, we want new hires to have met with all of the key stakeholders, gotten the lay of the land, built a first draft of their 30/60/90 plan, and shared it with relevant parties for feedback.

We suggest that their plan includes a quick win, one that can be shipped in the second week.

The first and second weeks are critical because they show the new hire *this is our culture*. This is how we behave. If we expect the new hire to ship the second week, this will set the pace for the new hire. Conversely, if we set a goal for the new hire to ship in 90 days, that will be the baseline expectation of the new hire moving forward.

Second week

Week two is for working! New hires get their managers to sign off on their 30/60/90, then publish it in their team's Slack channel.

As a manager, your job is to help your new hire with their first shippable project, ideally shipped before the end of this week. Expect that your new hire will be spending a large portion of this week reading, in one-on-ones, and still learning a ton.

First 30 days

Focus on shipping the 30/60/90. Hopefully your new hire has completed their first quick win in week two! If they have, have them post it to the *#shipped* channel.

It's important to remember that your new hire is still being interviewed 30 days in. You'll have had a first chance to work together and gather data that's impossible to ascertain during the formal interview process.

Be asking yourself:

1. Is everyone in the team still excited to have this person join?

2. Has this person displayed some of our cultural values and behaviors?

3. Have we given them feedback? What was the reaction?

4. What is their reaction to adversity?

Make sure to collect feedback from the new hire throughout the one-on-one check-ins to figure out what can be improved in the onboarding process. Every new hire should have an increasingly better experience.

First 90 days

At this point, your new hire should be onboarded. However, don't confuse this with "fully ramped." It will take three to six months for most people to gain enough context to start functioning at full capacity.

3. COACHING & FEEDBACK

Zone of Genius

Matching people to what needs to get done is an age-old problem in company building. And on a micro level, aligning yourself with the right role is also challenging. What should you delegate? Where should you focus your efforts?

Finding the right role must be an optimization between what you want, what you are good at, and what the organization needs now in order to achieve its goals, which in turn puts it into a path to achieve its mission.

We've found the Zone of Genius framework from The Big Leap [*bit.ly/ big-leap-book*] by Gay Hendricks to be a useful way of ensuring there's harmony between jobs and people. It's pretty straightforward, here's how it works.

The zones

There are four zones: Zone of Incompetence, Zone of Competence, Zone of Excellence, and Zone of Genius.

People's performance consists of a mixture of skills, strengths, and talents. Here's how we define them:

- A *strength* is anything that gives you energy.

* A *talent* is an innate ability that can't be taught (for example, being incredible with numbers).

* A *skill* is a competency that can be taught (for example, knowing Excel back to front).

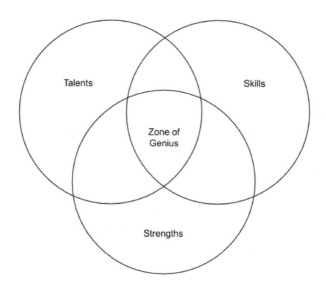

Zone of Incompetence

The most obvious misalignment between people and tasks is where there is a lack of talent or skills. In this case, the person should either be retrained, redistributed in the organization, or asked to find a better match outside the company.

Zone of Competence

These are tasks that people are good at, but that other people can do better. Work that falls under this category should be delegated or redistributed to people more suited for it.

Zone of Excellence

It's less clear when someone is talented and skilled in a particular area but the work doesn't give them energy. They may be successful in the short term, but over time they will burn out. We call this the Zone of Excellence. It's important to recognize when people are in this (or even better if *they* can recognize it) so you can do something about it.

Zone of Genius

When all talents, skills, and strengths are all aligned, we are in our Zone of Genius.

The things in your Zone of Genius are the things that you are uniquely good at in the world, and that you love to do (so much so, that time and space likely disappear when you do them). This is where you can add most value to the world and yourself. This is where you should be driving toward spending most, if not all, of your time. The same goes for your team; they're at their best when they're operating out of this place.

 "Some people worry that if each of us operates solely in our Zone of Genius, no one will be available to do the un-fun stuff. This is a false fear. There are many personality types. For every activity that feels un-fun to you, there is someone out there who not only excels at it, but loves it. The key in any organization is for people to be transparent about what their Zone of Genius is, and then map all activities to the right people through Areas of Responsibility (AORs)."

— Matt Mochary, The Great CEO Within

Feedback and the Zone of Genius

Every person is unique. You can't turn weaknesses into strengths, or create talent where there is none. These things are innate. All you can teach is skills and self-awareness, so direct your feedback there. Focus on doubling down on someone's existing Zone of Genius, or shift them into a role better aligned with their Zone of Genius.

Feedback

A good feedback system is an absolutely critical aspect of a functioning organization. At a macro level, when companies don't do feedback well, pockets of disagreements within organizations grow, causing resentment, distrust, and ultimately organizational failure. At a micro level, feedback is the only way to achieve true personal growth. You are not objective enough about yourself to grow effectively without external feedback.

> "If you avoid conflict to keep peace, you start a war inside yourself."
>
> —Someone wise

If feedback is so critical to a company's success, why do so many companies fail at it? In our experience, they fall short in three main areas: training to give feedback, training to receive feedback, and making it part of the culture. Ultimately, giving and receiving feedback is just hard; it often triggers painful emotions. The alternative, though, is failure. There's no such thing as a workplace without feedback. If you're not hearing "bad news," people are too afraid to give feedback to you and each other.

Giving feedback

Giving and receiving effective feedback is a skill like any other, and it needs to be part of your on-boarding training if your team is going to be any good at it.

Fortunately, there are some excellent resources like Nonviolent Communication and Conscious Leadership that provide a good structure to do it.

* Feedback should be given in private and regularly (i.e., weekly) at a time when someone is expecting it.

* Use Radical Candor, care personally, and challenge directly. Beware of *ruinous empathy* (see Common management mistakes).

* Feedback should come from a place of love and good intentions.

* Feedback should be specific and avoid sweeping statements, judgements, or labeling (e.g., avoid saying "I think you're lazy").

* Feedback should be in a nonviolent communication format (provided below).

The key to giving feedback is to prevent activating people's "lizard brain" and provoking a feeling of anger or fear. Base emotions, like fear and anger, are powerful; once invoked they cloud higher-level thought.

The good news is there's a simple way of communicating feedback that avoids provoking anger and defensiveness. First, ask *"is now is a good time for you for some feedback?"*, assuming yes proceed with:

 "When you do *specific action*, I feel *emotion* because the story in my head is *fear.*

Ensure that specific action is a fact, something that a camera would record. Emotion should be a core emotion, like anger, sadness, or fear. Don't avoid being vulnerable when describing your fear, make it as real and raw as possible. But also bear in mind that this is just a story in your head—other people may see situations differently and have different stories.

Wait for a response. It's important that whoever you're giving the feedback feels heard, and has a chance to clear up any stories you may have about them. Repeat back what they say to prove you've heard them. Then, end with a request:

 "My request is ____. Can you do that for me?"

So, a full example might be:

"When you didn't write any tests for that pull request you submitted last week, I feel fear because the story in my head is that you don't place enough value on testing, and that without tests we will introduce bugs that will upset customers, affect revenue, and ultimately destroy our chances of creating a successful company. .... My request is that you write tests for every pull request you submit. Can you do that for me?"

Positive feedback

It is just as important to give positive feedback as it is to give critical feedback. You will find that some people need more positive feedback than others, and some people love public praise, whereas others don't.

As with critical feedback, keep your praise specific. Otherwise you run the risk of operating in the quadrant of manipulative insincerity (see Radical Candor), which your report is going to see through.

For example:

 "When you did *specific action*, I felt joy because the knock-on effect for the company meant ..."

 "The research shows that people generally are more likely to act on specific positive feedback than on any other type of feedback. I liken feedback giving between two people to building a bank account. You're depositing specific positive feedback into the account so that you can make a withdrawal when you need to and still stay in the black. You never want to be in a relationship with someone where the negative feedback outweighs the positive. The research shows anywhere from 3 to 5 positives to every 1 negative is the optimal ratio to maintain healthy relationships and get people to act on your feedback."

— Abby Reider, LifeLabs Learning

Receiving feedback

The reason why you feel that knot in your stomach whenever you are about to receive feedback is that your ego views it as an attack, provoking a fight, flight, or freeze response. Your ego thinks you're about to be killed—it's no wonder you feel nervous!

The key is to learn to evaluate ideas objectively and view feedback as a gift. Now this is easier said than done, and will require constant effort and practice. We definitely recommend reading the two books mentioned above, but here's a little shortcut.

When people are giving you critical feedback, as soon as they're finished, repeat back to them what you heard. Say "What I'm hearing is XYZ. Is that right?" It is important that the person giving feedback knows that you're hearing and listening to them. Not only will this mechanism do that, but it will also ensure that you have some breathing time to think. Keep asking, "Is that all?" and repeating back until you're sure you've squeezed every last ounce of feedback out of them.

Now, take that piece of feedback and take a second to think about it objectively. Be curious, run through the possibilities. Even if you don't agree with all of it, or with the format in which it was delivered, are there aspects of it that you can take to improve yourself? If you accept the feedback, suggest an action to resolve it. Thank them—giving feedback isn't easy, and by doing so, they've shown they care about you. You don't have to accept all the feedback you're given, but at least give a good explanation why not (and be curious to how the opposite might be true).

Making it part of our culture

As a manager, it is your responsibility to set a good example and ensure that giving and receiving regular feedback is part of our culture. We do not leave it to an annual performance review. People should not be in the dark all year as to their performance. Furthermore, tying feedback to compensation is the best way to politicize it.

There is a simple way to achieve this: make it part of your team's weekly one-on-ones. Have a structured section at the end of a one-on-one for mutual feedback giving. Make sure that it's a requirement of all your managers, and ensure that it's recorded somewhere (we use Asana). To reiterate, giving positive feedback is just as important as critical feedback.

Lastly, publicly seek feedback from your team and discuss it. It sets a good example and demonstrates you're willing to be vulnerable and committed to growing.

"The leadership team gives me written feedback at our meetings, which I take and publish to the entire company. I address the feedback and discuss ways I'm trying to improve. Not only does this demonstrate a degree of vulnerability, but if people see that you view feedback as a gift, they will start doing likewise."

— *Alex MacCaw*

Feedback and power dynamics

While we have tried to instill a culture of mutual feedback-giving at Clearbit, we have struggled to elicit critical feedback given upwards from a report to their manager. Although this is understandable, it's far from ideal. Feedback is critical for the growth of both parties.

We are tackling this in a number of ways through training, anonymous feedback, and surveys, but it is an ongoing effort.

As a manager, you need to ensure that your reports feel safe giving you feedback, and that it's worth their time. Trust builds over time. If your report sees you react positively to critical feedback by taking action, they're more likely to give you more in the future. And they're more likely to be candid.

It's important to close the loop on critical feedback you're given. If you decide to act on it, do so quickly and update your report at the next opportunity. If you don't decide to act on it, explain why. But whatever you do, don't treat feedback with silence.

Anonymous Feedback

At Clearbit, we have a culture of giving and receiving feedback, because it's one of the best ways of promoting self-growth. Ideally we can always put our name to feedback, but it's also important that we have an outlet for anonymous feedback. This is useful because:

* It allows us to collect feedback in aggregate and survey employees

* It lets people be candid when they perhaps otherwise wouldn't

* It encourages us to focus on the message, not the messenger

We use TinyPulse [*app.tinypulse.com*] to survey everyone by email weekly. We encourage everyone to fill out the survey, we look at it every week, and the results go directly into practice. We also periodically publish the aggregate results.

Every response submitted to TinyPulse **is anonymous,** and messages are viewable only by the Leadership team. The only breakdown we see is which department the respondent is in.

Every month we ask the question "How happy are you at work?" You can think of this as an internal NPS score, and we use this to track team happiness over time. This gives us an early warning indication to issues (like scaling too rapidly).

Generally, when there is a significant issue, we do an all-hands results evaluation with the results and proposed solutions. For example, a survey showed that one of the most draining aspects of Clearbit was ineffective meetings. In response to this, we created a new meeting structure (see Running meetings) and stricter policies as to when meetings can be created.

Questions we've asked in the past include:

- What is the most challenging aspect of giving/receiving feedback at Clearbit, and how can we help the company get better at it?

- Do you feel like you have the opportunity to reach your full potential at our organization?

- How can we improve our remote work culture?

- How can the leadership team improve?

- What are Clearbit's blind spots?

- Do you know what is expected of you at work?

- How do you feel about Alex's performance as CEO? What are some areas he could improve on?

- What did you like best at your previous employment that you'd like to see implemented here?

- How likely are you to refer a friend to work here?

If you find that answers given in anonymous feedback surprise you and don't reflect one-on-one feedback, it may indicate a lack of receptivity to feedback from your leadership, or a deeper issue.

 Radical Candor

In Radical Candor [*radicalcandor.com*], Kim Scott outlines the different types of feedback that managers give, and the traps you can fall into when doing so. She has developed a system for giving effective feedback outlined below.

The TLDR is:

- Ideally, first build a relationship with anyone before giving them feedback. Make sure they know you care personally about them and their career.
- Then be extremely candid and clear with your critical feedback. Leave no room for interpretation.
- Do not sugarcoat feedback to make people feel better.
- Do not get personal or make sweeping statements. Be specific.
- Be humble. If you are wrong, you want to know.
- For positive feedback, be just as specific. Otherwise you're just being insincere.

The following are excerpts taken from Kim's book, Radical Candor.

The four quadrants

The four quadrants of feedback are Ruinous Empathy (the most common mistake), Manipulative Insincerity, Obnoxious Aggression, and Radical Candor.

Manipulative Insincerity

 "People give praise and criticism that is manipulatively insincere when they are too focused on being liked or think they can gain some sort of political advantage by being fake—or when they are just too tired to care or argue any more.When you are overly worried about how people will perceive you, you're less willing to say what needs to be said."

— *Kim Scott, Radical Candor*

Feedback that is manipulatively insincere rarely reflects what the speaker actually thinks; rather, it's an attempt to push the other person's emotional buttons in return for some personal gain. Manipulatively insincere feedback happens when you don't care enough about a person to challenge directly.

Obnoxious Aggression

When you criticize someone without taking time to show you care about them personally, your feedback feels obnoxiously aggressive to the recipient.

When managers belittle employees, embarrass them publicly, or freeze them out, their behavior falls into this quadrant.

 "Obnoxious Aggression sometimes gets great results short-term but leaves a trail of dead bodies in its wake in the long run."

— *Kim Scott, Radical Candor*

Often Obnoxious Aggression stems from fear. Fear of rejection. Fear of anyone questioning your authority. If you find yourself shutting people down, look inside and figure out what fear is driving that response.

An example of obnoxious aggression would be:

"You didn't prepare an update for our one-on-one, Alex; quite frankly, I think you're incompetent!"

Ruinous Empathy

Ruinous empathy is the most common mistake people make when giving feedback. Managers sugarcoat feedback in an attempt to make it land better, but in reality they dilute the message and undermine the feedback. What's worse is that sometimes managers use ruinous empathy to justify not giving feedback at all!

 "There's a Russian anecdote about a guy who has to amputate his dog's tail but loves him so much that he cuts it off an inch each day, rather than all at once. His desire to spare the dog pain and suffering only leads to more pain and suffering. Don't allow yourself to become that kind of manager!"

— Kim Scott, Radical Candor

We sometimes hear people say, "I didn't say exactly that, but they definitely knew what I meant." Well, no one can read your mind. It's much easier to say exactly what you mean to say and remove all room for interpretation.

 "Managers rarely intend to ruin an employee's chance of success or to handicap the entire team by letting poor performance slide. And yet, that is often the net result of Ruinous

Empathy. Similarly, praise that's ruinously empathetic is not effective because its primary goal is to make the person feel better rather than to point out really great work and push for more of it.

Ruinous Empathy can also prevent a manager from asking for criticism. Typically, when a manager asks an employee for criticism, the employee feels awkward at best, afraid at worst. Instead of pushing through the discomfort to get an employee to challenge them, managers who are being ruinously empathetic may be so eager to ease the awkwardness that they simply let the matter drop.

Managers often make the mistake of thinking that if they hang out in the Ruinous Empathy quadrant, they can build a relationship with their direct reports and then move over to Radical Candor. They're pleasant to work with, but as time goes by, their employees start to realize that the only feedback they've received is "good job" and other vaguely positive comments. They know they've done some things wrong, but they're not sure what, exactly. Their direct reports never know where they stand, and they aren't being given an opportunity to learn or grow; they often stall or get fired. Not such a great way to build a relationship."

— *Kim Scott, Radical Candor*

An example of ruinous empathy might be:

"When we put typos in emails to customers, it doesn't look quite as professional as we should. I know you're super busy, I totally get why this happens, but I'm hoping we can all make more of an effort."

Radical Candor

"Radical Candor" is what happens when you put "Care Personally" and "Challenge Directly" together.

People will believe that you care personally when they trust you and believe you have their best interests at heart. This will only happen if you forge a deep personal connection with them. Take the time to really get to know everyone on your team, their strengths, their weaknesses, their desires out of life. Realize we are all human beings, with human feelings, and even at work, we need to be seen as such.

Then communicate feedback clearly and candidly. Do not beat around the bush or sugarcoat feedback. You will only water down the message, serving no one. You need to give feedback that, in a way, does not call into question your confidence in their abilities but leaves no room for interpretation.

 "Candid feedback is offered humbly. Implicit with candor is that you're simply offering your view of what's going on and that you expect people to offer theirs. If it turns out that in fact you're the one who got it wrong, you want to know. You are giving the other person insight into your internal story about them and offering them a chance to change it.

It turns out that when people trust you and believe you care about them, they are much more likely to:

1. Accept and act on your praise and criticism

2. Tell you what they really think about what you are doing well and, more importantly, not doing so well

3. Engage in this same behavior with one another

4. Embrace their role on the team

5. Focus on getting results

The most surprising thing about Radical Candor may be that its results are often the opposite of what you fear. You fear people will become angry or vindictive; instead they are usually grateful for the chance to talk it through. And even when you do get that initial anger, resentment, or sullenness, those emotions prove to be fleeting when the person knows you really care."

— *Kim Scott, Radical Candor*

An example of radical candor might be:

"The widget feature is now 30 days delayed after the mutually agreed-upon deadline. This makes me feel fear because the story in my head is that you don't appreciate deadlines. The rest of the marketing and sales team are geared around this deadline, and missing it causes a lot of disruption. Further still, if we don't have a culture of keeping to our commitments, I fear that ultimately we will be slow to ship products, fail to raise a round, the company will go bankrupt, and everyone will lose their jobs. In the future, can you keep your commitments and deadlines?"

What happens in cases where you don't have a personal connection with someone but still have candid feedback to give them? Give it to them anyway, with the same candor. It may upset them in the short term, but in the long term you will build that relationship and they will understand you are giving them feedback to try and help them.

An example of asking to give feedback to someone who you don't yet have a relationship with:
"You are extremely valuable to Clearbit (or another group), and

Feedback rewrites

Providing ineffective feedback is one of the most common mistakes we see managers make. Time and time again, we see managers operating with ruinous empathy rather than being radically candid.

This is why we spend so much time during our manager training focused on good feedback. It's also why we regularly audit the feedback our managers are giving. Below are some examples of real feedback, and how we would rewrite it.

Before (ruinous empathy):

"I wish we had taken more time to test the widget feature better. It seems that a lot of the issues we had could have been prevented by better testing in dev; if we had a better environment in there, it would help as well. I'll talk to sysops about it and start thinking on it. Would be great for us to build a culture of testing things better early on locally and in dev before moving to staging and production."

Notice the ruinous empathist uses the word "we," rather than being direct. They also beat around the bush, not directly addressing the issue, and start making excuses for the report.

Let's rewrite that with some radical candor:

"The widget feature had a number of bugs in it which caused two customer complaints. It looks like you didn't write any tests for it. When you don't take the time to test, I get scared because the story in my head is that you don't care about testing which is going to cause more bugs, decrease our

shipping speed, and ultimately could make this new product fail. Can you ensure that the work you're doing in the future is well tested?"

Notice how direct that is. The manager speaks in inarguable truths and demonstrates some vulnerability.

Let's take a look at another example. First, the ruinous empathy:

"I wish we had communicated better around the Facebook fix. It feels like you never got to prioritize it after our conversation. If we had discussed it earlier, maybe I could have that assigned to someone else. Nothing huge, but probably something we can learn from."

Notice the use of "we" again, and "feels like" to refer to something that isn't a feeling. Also notice the weasel get-out excuse baked right in (presumably to make them feel better). Let's try a rewrite:

"When you said you would prioritize fixing that bug with Facebook, and never created a prioritization card in Asana, I felt scared. The story in my head is that you don't understand how important it is to the company we get this fixed, and you do not think it is important to keep to your commitments. Going forward, when you agree to something, can you do it?"

👥 Running one-on-ones

The one-on-one is your most important meeting as a manager. They are the focal point of your team's relationship with you, and they are your best point of leverage to enact any changes you want to make.

When we talk to managers outside of Clearbit, one of the first questions we ask is how they run one-on-ones. Surprisingly, most have no system; instead, they run ad hoc, unstructured one-on-one meetings (often with hand-wavy justifications).

In our experience, this is a mistake. A one-on-one should be prepared for and highly structured to make the most use of the time available. This might seem onerous at first, but over time you will realize that the opposite is true; the structure is freeing. It lets you get the mundane topics quickly out of the way, and then focus on more blue-sky thinking.

The purpose of a one-on-one

A one-on-one serves a few purposes:

1. Relationship building, creating an atmosphere of trust between you and your team, where it's clear that you care personally about them

2. Feedback giving and receiving, so people understand how they're performing and their areas of growth. This goes for you as well – if you're not getting feedback, then elicit it!

3. Information sharing, especially highlighting the status of immediate goals. Most of this can be pre-written (and even pre-read) to save time.

4. Top tasks accountability, ensuring that people do what they have committed to doing by being an accountability partner (rather than a micro-manager).

5. Career growth, talking through people's aspirations and helping them get there

Effective one-on-ones are like immune systems for companies. They're critical for bubbling up and resolving issues that could otherwise spiral out of control. They're also crucial in giving feedback to people so everyone is clear on how they're performing.

Asking questions

Remember, one-on-ones aren't there for you to micromanage your team. Instead, you should be a sounding board that your team can use to bounce ideas off and come up with their own solutions. **Ask questions rather than make statements.** Help people come to their own conclusions; it's the only way they'll truly become independent.

"When the supervisor thinks the subordinate has said all he wants to about a subject, he should ask another question. He should try to keep the flow of thoughts coming by prompting the subordinate with queries until both feel satisfied they have gotten to the bottom of the problem."

— *Andy Grove, High Output Management*

The Coaching Habit [*bit.ly/coachinghabit-stanier*] suggest six questions you can ask to help stimulate the conversation:

1. The kick-start question: "What's on your mind?"

2. The AWE question: "And what else?"

3. The focus question: "What's the real challenge here for you?"

4. The foundation question: "And what do YOU want?"

5. The lazy question: "How can I help?"

6. The strategic question: "If you're saying YES to this, what are you saying NO to?"

7. The learning question: "What was most useful for you?"

Accountability

When people commit to doing something, it's very important that you hold them accountable to that. Ensure that any commitment is written down in Asana with an owner and a due date to remove all disambiguation. We call these Impeccable agreements.

You are your team's accountability partner. Make it clear that broken commitments are not acceptable.

Since they are now committed to keeping all of their agreements, it's very important for them to be careful about the things they say "yes" to. If they agree to too many things, they will stretch themselves in a way that will result in broken agreements.

Organizing one-on-ones

The first one-on-one meeting should occur soon after the onboarding process is complete. We recommend starting with a recurring 30-minute meeting every week; you can always make it longer down the road, if required.

We recommend doing all of your one-on-ones back to back on a single day. This is efficient, requires less context switching, and allows you to spot patterns you might otherwise miss.

The maximum amount of direct reports is seven. More than that, and you're going to spend all your time in one-on-ones.

Setup

We are using Asana to track one-on-ones. Use our Asana template [*bit. ly/1-1template*] to create a new project and give access to both the manager and the team member. We recommend using the naming convention *Manager / Employee*.

It looks like this:

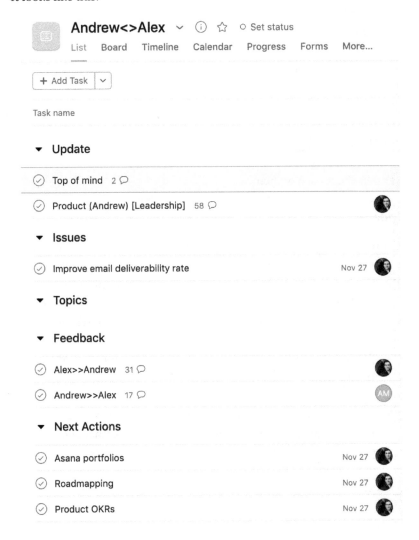

Preparation

The key to running an effective one-on-one is preparation. This lets you run your one-on-ones in 30 minutes, whizz through procedural work, and get to the more meaty topics (where the fun happens).

The four parts of preparing a one-on-one are:

1. Update

2. Issues & proposed solutions

3. Topic

4. Feedback

Let's talk about each of them.

Update

Your report will pre-write an update detailing what has happened since the last one-on-one. Updates should be added as comments to the Update task. Create a commitment with your report to do this every week prior to the one-on-one. Ideally, the update should include "what went well" and "what could improve," grouped around your report's OKRs.

1. Track progress toward KPIs. Any KPI that's lagging should be turned into an issue below.

2. Bubble up any pertinent information about how your goals have gone (e.g., What new information did you gather about the customer? The product?).

Here's an sample update from our Growth team:

💡 O1: Sprint toward Q4 revenue goal

Good:

- HubSpot integration launch went well. Achieved 95% of target leads.

- Dynamic Forms Webinar pushed 100 leads

- Homepage A/B test going live today

Bad:

- We have 2-3 more weeks to drive Q4 demand. Feels like we're not on track to hit our goals.

- Moving blog to primary domain is proving to be a PITA

- Shipped some sloppy copy / assets in the sprint

This update will be read in silence at the beginning of the one-on-one (or even better, pre-read) so that everyone is synchronized on the state of the company. Once you get in the habit of pre-written work, you can even read updates prior to the meeting (and comment on them) to save time.

Issues and proposed solutions

Issues are typically things that are blocking your reports' work and need your assistance or insight.

Any issues that crop up should be written up in the issue style and created as Asana tasks under the Issues section. Ideally, they also have a proposed solution that you can quickly approve. For example:

Issue

Leadership team is not putting expenses in the right category from their corporate credit cards. This is causing lots of extra admin overhead for our accounting team.

Proposed solution

Leadership team moves entirely onto Airbase [*airbase.com*] (should have already received physical cards).

Topics

Topics are open-ended points of discussion that your report wants to cover. This is usually where the magic happens, where blue-sky thinking flows, and where creativity is unleashed.

Prompt your report to create topics prior to the meeting. This will encourage some prep work and time to think from both parties.

Topics should have a good description that you can quickly read to gain context, but not necessarily contain a conclusion.

Feedback

Ideally, feedback should be prepared beforehand by both parties. This allows for more considered feedback rather than off-the-cuff ideas. But, even if you haven't prepared anything, still make sure you do it at the end of the one-on-one.

Feedback should be in the *Like that / Wish that* format.

1. **Like that...** Say what you liked about the team member's actions since the previous meeting? Be specific. During the week, actively look for actions to compliment.

2. **Wish that...** What do you wish would change? Be as specific and vulnerable as possible.

3. **It's required that...** behavior that needs to change/improve, otherwise the next step is Performance improvement plans (PIP).

We separated out '*wish that*' feedback and critical PIP level feedback because we were finding that some people were constantly afraid they were going to be put on a PIP.

It is important to also elicit negative feedback about your or the company's actions. Do this any way you can, be very thankful for it, and then act to resolve the stated issues quickly. This is the key to making a team member feel heard and valued.

While we have a culture of feedback, we have found it difficult to elicit feedback from reports back to their managers. When asking for feedback, be sure to leave several seconds so the other person has time to think and respond, versus feeling the urge to close the awkward silence too soon.

Read our chapter dedicated to feedback before giving or receiving any feedback: Feedback.

Format

Run one-on-one meetings according to the following template.

1. Kick off the meeting by asking your team member about the highlight of their week. This doesn't need to be restricted to work; anything will do. This gets everyone in a great headspace and builds on your relationship.

2. Then read your team member's prepared update in silence. Read the entire thing before asking any questions. This update should

be grouped around their OKRs for the quarter, and be split into "what went well" and "what could improve" sections around each objective.

3. Next, go through your team member's issues (and proposed solutions). Try to keep to a few minutes for each issue and not get bogged down in minutiae. For clear asks, give an immediate response or create a follow-up task. Otherwise, we recommend helping people come to their own conclusions, which will foster a sense of healthy independence.

4. Next, talk about topics. These are more open-ended discussions and time for blue-sky thinking.

5. Now ask, "What are the three most important things you want to get done by this time next week?" Remember, ideally you are not telling people what to do; they should get used to figuring this out for themselves. Preferably whatever they come up with should be related to their OKRs. Jot down the three tasks in Asana, and set the owner and due date for the next one-on-one. Hold people accountable. If tasks are not completed, ask why, and then ask for a "habit" so that this never happens again. This ensures that your team is working to a regular accountability cadence, and it encourages their minds to be focused on their top priorities.

6. Lastly comes feedback. We have written a whole chapter on this (), but the key aspect is that if there is any critical feedback, there is mutual trust that it will be shared.

7. Then high-five. This seals any commitments and leaves the meeting on a good note.

Name	Duration
Highlight of the week	2 minutes

Name	Duration
Read prepared update (in silence)	5 minutes
Questions regarding update	3 minutes
Issues & proposed solutions	5 minutes
Topics	5 minutes
Top tasks	5 minutes
Prepared feedback	5 minutes
High five	

⚒ Professional development

The goal of professional development is to help your people accomplish their growth goals and, in doing so, improve your team's performance. Each member of your team should become clear around their own values, talents, skills, knowledge, and goals. Once they have that level of self-awareness, they should understand in detail what the next steps are for developing those traits and achieving their goals.

Your job is to guide them to the answer themselves. Then, once you understand where employees are trying to go, you can make adjustments in their current role to move them in the right direction. This knowledge will also shape the feedback you're giving them.

You should have a distinct understanding of the future plans of everyone on your team. Do they want to become a senior engineer, transition from SDR or AE, or start their own business? To grow is human. If we don't provide an environment where people feel like they can grow, they will simply leave.

A great place to discuss this is in your team's one-on-ones. We recommend having a professional development conversation at least once every quarter.

> It's important to remember that Clearbit is just a phase in people's lives. At some point everyone currently working at Clearbit will leave. Indeed, at some point, Clearbit won't exist! Our goal is to try and make it one of the best phases of people's lives, and set them up for whatever they want to do next.

Talking about Clearbit as a phase is an important idea to convey to your report before they share their career goals because most folks are used to keeping their true goals hidden lest they are looked upon as disloyal or having conflicting goals with the company. The manager-employee relationship is really a symbiotic one: the employee creates value for the company in exchange for growth opportunities that may or may not continue at the company.

Growth doesn't have to be at work

You may find that your report is quite happy in their current role and career. Perhaps they are focused on areas outside of work. That's totally fine. Don't force your definition of growth down their throats. If someone is doing great work for the company, and they're happy doing just that, let them do their thing.

Growth doesn't have to be an up-level progression

Growth is really learning new skills. You can grow by learning peripheral skills that interest you; e.g., as a back-end engineer, you can grow by learning distributed systems design (go deeper) or by learning front-end development or marketing (go broader).

These skills don't necessarily advance you to the next compensation level if the skills are not highly valued in your role. But you may still highly value the skills yourself because you want to found your own startup later. (This is also why being explicit about supporting the employee's career goal up front is critical.)

The up-level progression is simply a recognition of your achievement of mastery in a set of skills highly valued in your current role and the impact that the new role will have.

Growth is not management

For whatever reason, our society drills into us that to have career growth, we need to go into management. This is absolutely not the case. If your report wants to go into management, great—but that's not a promotion, that's a career change.

Management requires a totally different skill set. If you have a report adamant on going into management, start discussing how to grow that skill set with them first. For a start, they should know this handbook back to front.

Leveling system

Career discussions are not promotion discussions. The trouble with bringing conversations back to compensation is that it promotes short-term thinking. A career is a decades-long endeavor that surpasses any one company's corporate ladder.

That said, for better or for worse, we do have a leveling system. If someone wants to get paid more at Clearbit, they will need to move up in the leveling system (not necessarily directly up, but possibly also up via a lateral move).

Why do we have a leveling system? It's the best answer we've come up with to make compensation objective and fair. It is far from perfect, though. Don't confuse the levels that we've made up with steps in your career. It's a rigid system that doesn't pretend to encompass the richness of someone's life.

Every department maintains their leveling system (which you can find in our wiki). Here's an example of the various levels in Engineering [*bit.ly/ eng-roles*] that we are currently hiring for:

- Software Engineer (IC2)

    » Write readable, tested, idiomatic code *(e.g., good structure, following code style)*

    » Apply relevant knowledge, tools, and techniques *(e.g., using background queues to buffer writes)*

    » and so on...

- Sr. Software Engineer (IC3)

    » Lead substantial technical projects *(e.g., scope, track, deliver on requirements)*

    » Identify and resolve ambiguous technical issues (e.g., use tracing to debug request lifecycle)

    » and so on...

- Principal Software Engineer (IC4)

    » Strong individual contributor and technical leader (including everything for Sr. Software Engineer)

    » Support other team members on technical issues

    » Establish team technical policies (in harmony with the rest of Clearbit Engineering)

    » and so on...

* Engineering Manager (M3)

  » Run standups, retrospectives, and other team meetings where needed

  » Provide continuous feedback and regular performance assessment

  » and so on...

Notice that we have an IC4 level that's higher than the manager level. It's important that we have IC levels that are equal to or higher than manager levels, otherwise you're signaling that the only way to get promoted is to go into management.

Having a discussion

Your professional development discussion should revolve around an 18-month plan and a longer vision. Ask your report to come to your one-on-one prepared with answers to the following questions:

* How would you describe your success in your current role?

* What do you actually do that makes you as good as you are?

* Which part of your current role do you enjoy most?

* How does professional success intersect with personal happiness in the context of your current role? Do you think it's achievable? Why/why not?

* What would be the perfect role for you?

* What goals (inside and outside of work) do you have over the next 18 months?

- What would you like to be doing five years from now?

- Write down five to ten skills or competencies you think are required to get to this place, and then rate yourself on each of these on a scale of 1–10.

Since this is all prepared, you can do some thinking of your own prior to the meeting. The first thing to consider is self-awareness. Has your report listed all the skills and competencies required to get to where they want to be, and how does their competency rating compare to your impression of them?

If there's a lack of self-awareness, ask your report if they'd be interested in seeing your scores for them for each skill and competency. While this can be a tricky conversation, the alternative is doing them a disservice by not opening their eyes to any blind spots.

Lastly, ask your report for ideas on how to work on developing these areas. It's much better if the ideas come from them! Try to morph their role and incorporate growth in the areas they're interested in.

Mentorship

Mentors can be a powerful way of catalyzing personal growth. You should be a mentor to your team, but it's also helpful to look for additional mentors outside of the company.

In Coaching, we talked about setting up an advisory board of three to five people who have experience in your domain and have committed to helping you. The difference between an advisor and a mentor is that an advisor directs and a mentor guides. Advisors have such deep domain knowledge that you can ask specific technical questions. Mentors should have a deeper understanding of what in particular motivates you, and they should serve more as a sounding board. Both roles have their place.

We suggest working with your reports to set up similar support structures for them. Prompt your team to look in their network for people who can serve as mentors, and if you have anyone relevant in your network, offer an introduction.

Personal coaching

An alternative to being mentored is using a personal coach. The leadership team at Clearbit all have coaches via a service called Torch [*torch.io*]. We also extend life coaching services to the entire team through Modern Health [*joinmodernhealth.com*].

Taking responsibility for your own growth

Ultimately the ownership for career growth lies with the employee (not the manager). While this idea can be counterintuitive for a lot of people, acknowledging it is the only path to true growth.

Managers and the company are there to provide opportunities and shortcuts to growth. They have opportunities to apply in the real world some skill, or experts that have done it before to ask questions of. But they don't own growth; the employee owns it.

This means that an employee, not their manager, should be in the driver's seat about their own career. An employee should seek clarity around what they want to learn next and jointly work with their manager to seek out those things.

Unfortunately, it's all too common for folks to expect their manager to tell them how they should grow next. While it's important to explain our ladder and what the company needs, it's just as important to bounce the question back to your report: What do *they* want out of their life?

Common management mistakes

As a manager, it's only inevitable that you're going to make mistakes. The important thing is to learn from them, improve, and move on. However, there are mistakes that we see people make time and time again.

Heroing

The most common mistake we see in managers is "heroing." That is doing the work of your subordinates on their behalf.

You may think you are being "nice" by lending a hand, but you are actually perpetuating the problem by not setting your team up for long-term success.

More often than not, this stems from an issue of trust. You don't trust that the work will be done up to your level of quality. Sometimes this is true; after all, you have probably been at the company for years and built up institutional knowledge. However, as long as you continue to badly delegate, then this will continue to be true and your team won't have a chance to learn.

There are a few ways to think about this. Is your lack of trust in their ability due to an issue with effective training, or did you make the wrong hire?

If it is due to a lack of training, then consider whether this might be a great opportunity for your team member to gain experience. If the work isn't mission critical, delegate it and monitor what happens. Provide feedback and iterate. The extra effort is worth it in the long term.

If the team member is a wrong fit, then consider making a change. The longer you wait, the longer this problem will persist because you will spend all your time doing IC work rather than recruiting.

Is it ok to "hero"?

In a perfect system, we should never have to "hero." Everyone has their designated work and they delegate effectively. However, there will be extenuating circumstances that require someone to step in once in a while (especially in a startup). In these cases, it is okay to "hero"—the key thing to remember is to make it obvious to everyone that you are "heroing." Tell your team member that you will "hero" them once in this circumstance, but that they should come up with a habit to prevent this from happening again.

Not prioritizing hiring

Not hiring effectively is the other big mistake we see in management. Being excellent at hiring is a skill we require from all managers at Clearbit. Slow hiring leads to a vicious cycle of managers doing too much IC work, not having enough time to work on hiring, and then having to do more IC work.

The only way to break yourself out of this cycle is to pause your IC work and focus on hiring. It's clearly much better to preempt this and hire ahead of time.

Not acting fast enough when someone isn't working out

Time and time again, we see managers that drag their feet in firing people who clearly are not working out. It's important to remember that your team reflects on you. If you are not making a change that clearly needs to be made, it'll be noticed.

Not only that, you're also creating an unfair environment for the rest of the team because they are shouldering additional burden, not just because of the underperforming teammate, but also due to your indecisiveness.

Ruinous Empathy

As mentioned in the section on Radical Candor, we have found ruinous empathy to be the most common mistake managers make when giving feedback.

Ruinous empathy makes managers sugarcoat feedback in an attempt to make people feel better. Managers will often justify this to themselves because they think it'll make the feedback land better. In reality by doing this, they are diluting the message and undermining the feedback, helping no one.

What's worse is that sometimes managers use ruinous empathy to justify not giving feedback at all.

4. WORKING AS A TEAM

🤝 Impeccable agreements

Every day hundreds of agreements are made at Clearbit. These agreements are a key part of what makes Clearbit work. Agreements are made between two people (e.g., "I agree to complete project X by date Y") or with yourself (e.g., "I'm going to exercise three days a week").

It's important that we can trust each other to keep to our agreements. Imagine what would happen if we only kept to 80% of our agreements. You could safely assume that two out of ten agreements wouldn't be kept, but which two? You'd have to continually follow up and check on each agreement to see whether it had been missed or forgotten.

There's an automatic price you pay when you break an agreement: you disintegrate trust. The more agreements you break, the more you gain a reputation as someone who's unreliable. And unreliable people aren't trusted with important work.

This goes for agreements with others, but also for agreements with yourself. Think about the last agreement you broke with yourself. How does that make you feel? Anger? Shame? The story you should want to believe about yourself is that you are a reliable person who can achieve anything you set your mind to.

So, what's the solution? Impeccable agreements.

What is an "impeccable agreement"?

Every agreement between people at Clearbit should be impeccable. An impeccable agreement has the following properties:

1. It is recorded (we use Asana).

2. It is precisely defined (i.e., it has a comprehensive description, such that a third party could adjudicate if it was finished).

3. It has a specific due date.

Decide on OKRs

Assignee	matt
Due date	Jul 31, 2019
Projects	MattS<>Alex Done ⌄
Description	Discuss OKRs with the Growth team and create a final set of them.

Keeping an impeccable agreement means that we do everything we say we are going to do or we renegotiate the agreement if we no longer want to keep it.

Since we are now committed to keeping our agreements, it's now important to be careful about the things we say "yes" to. Don't agree to too many things, stretching yourself in a way that will result in broken agreements.

Renegotiating agreements

Life happens, priorities change, and sometimes agreements can't be kept. That's okay. The key is to renegotiate agreements as soon as you know you can't keep them. Contact the person you made the agreement with and explain the situation. Either push back the due date or cancel the agreement completely.

When and how you try to renegotiate an agreement can make a big difference (e.g., realizing the day before the due date that a big project isn't going to make it on time versus being able to spot this coming in advance).

What happens when agreements are broken

If an impeccable agreement has been broken without being renegotiated, there must be consequences.

 "The first time someone doesn't meet an agreement, you point it out to them immediately. If they apologize, you respond that apologies are not needed, and all that is required is that they only make agreements that they can commit to and that they meet all the agreements they make. If the person continues to fail at these, there is only one consequence that makes sense: they can no longer be part of the company."

— *Matt Mochary, The Great CEO Within*

Usually, when agreements are broken, there is a root cause, like poor prioritization. In these cases, we suggest creating a habit to make sure it never happens again; for example, adding a Top Task calendar event for an hour every day to ensure that important things get done. Another option is making this calendar event task specific, which is especially relevant for longer tasks.

Creating an accountability cadence

A great place to get people into the habit of keeping to their agreements is during their scheduled one-on-one. Run through their agreements (tasks assigned to them in Asana) and ensure that they've been kept.

Read more in our Running one-on-ones section.

Agreements with yourself

Keeping agreements with yourself is just as important as keeping agreements with others. Otherwise, how are you going to achieve your dreams and reach your potential? These tasks may seem small and insignificant, but every great journey starts with a single step.

By making small agreements with yourself, achieving them, and then making larger ones, you will start to develop a mindset that you can achieve anything you set your mind to. You will find that this is an incredibly powerful story to believe about yourself, and this will lead to greater success and personal happiness.

You can keep personal agreements either in Asana or in a personal to-do list like Things [*culturedcode.com/things*].

 Running meetings

Managing our time is one of the few truly zero-sum games we play. Since our minds are single-threaded and our lifespan limited, spending time on one thing necessitates not spending time on other things. In other words, there is an opportunity cost.

Meetings use time, ergo they are zero-sum too. For one meeting to exist, something else (usually another meeting) must be replaced. Therefore, two things are critical:

* Meetings must be kept to an absolute minimum.

* Any meeting that does happen must be rigorously managed to make optimal use of time.

We can't stress how important it is to get a handle on meetings. Whenever we see team burn-out, it is invariably due to an avalanche of meetings. Luckily, as with almost everything, we can use systems to save us.

Meetings TLDR

- Every meeting must have an owner (designated in the calendar invite).

- Only precisely the number of people who need to attend are invited.

- Clarify what kind of meeting it is before you start.

- The meeting owner must assign a note taker.

- Leave a meeting if you are giving or receiving no value.

Should we have a meeting?

There is a simple formula to determine how much a meeting costs:

```
number of participants * 200 * duration in hours
```

The *200* represents someone's hourly salary. For example, a five-person meeting lasting an hour would cost the company $1,000. This is the minimum cost, as the true cost will be much higher once you factor in opportunity cost.

Meetings are therefore incredibly expensive and should be avoided unless the return on investment is positive. Before creating a meeting, ask yourself whether a Slack message or a Google Doc will suffice instead.

You might ask yourself, if meetings are so expensive, why not ban them altogether? Unfortunately, this is not possible for the following reasons:

- Broadcast meetings are necessary because people don't read or notice everything.

- Some conversations need to be high bandwidth, so doing those asynchronously is inefficient.

- Brainstorming is facilitated by in-person riffing.

- Lastly, this is not a great reason, but meetings can force action.

Meeting types

There are a few different types of internal meetings:

- One-on-one meetings

- Staff meetings (recurring status updates, department sync, etc.)

- Decision meetings (one-off)

- All hands (information sharing and celebration)

- Training

Clarify what type of meeting you are having when it is created. Since we have already tackled how to run a one-on-one meeting (see Running one-on-ones, here we are going to focus on staff meetings and decision meetings. These are the two that tend to run amok anyhow.

Meeting attendees

Only precisely the right people who need to attend the meeting should be at the meeting. For a staff meeting, this is usually only key decision makers and the people who are providing updates.

If you need a specific person to attend a specific meeting, then don't add them to the recurring meeting. Just add them to the one they need to attend. Add them to the start of the agenda, so they can give or get value from that part of the meeting and then exit if the rest of the meeting doesn't give or get value from them.

 If you are not adding or receiving any value from a meeting, simply state, "Hey all, not sure I'm providing much value in this meeting. I'm going to step out." If someone does this in your meeting, don't read anything into it—it's Clearbit policy.

Meeting owners

The golden rule to meetings is that they **must have an owner**. This is a person who will emcee the meeting and be responsible for preparing for the meeting agenda, assigning a note taker, distributing notes post-meeting, and keeping everyone accountable for follow-up actions.

Meeting owners are expected to guide the conversation, cut off conversations that are spiraling out of control, postpone conversations that need more information, and ensure that people aren't distracting themselves with phones and email, while strictly keeping to the schedule.

It's important that everyone arrives on time for the meeting; otherwise, punctual people are left in limbo. As an owner, if you find that people are consistently late, create a task in the meeting's Asana project, recording who was on time and who wasn't.

The meeting owner must be specified in the meeting invite.

Note taking and recording

Why do people like being in meetings? Well, one reason is that it's only by being in the meeting that they are kept "in the loop." Thus they waste time going to a meeting when reading about the outcomes asynchronously could have sufficed.

Note taking solves that problem. Effective meeting notes summarize what was discussed in the meeting and what was decided. Notes can then be distributed to your team and read by anyone who wishes to so they don't feel left out. It's far more efficient for people to read a meeting summary than to sit through the meeting in person.

Distributing notes has the additional advantage of not rewarding managers with special information that individual contributors don't have access to. Information asymmetry is a hidden form of compensation and can make ICs want to become managers just to be "in the know."

It is difficult for most people to simultaneously think deeply and take notes. Therefore, at the start of the meeting, the meeting owner must designate a note taker for the meeting. This role should be rotated between meetings.

Notes are stored as comments on a dedicated "note" task in the Meetings project. Note takers are also responsible for recording any next-actions that the meeting owner wants to create in Asana. Every next action must be an impeccable agreement (see Impeccable agreements).

Almost every meeting at Clearbit is automatically recorded, transcribed, and available in Chorus.ai for the same reasons.

Meeting invites

Every meeting is born with an invite. Even at this early stage, things can start to go wrong.

First, ask yourself, "Is this meeting actually required?" because it's the first question that people you invite to the meeting will ask you. Can the meeting be replaced with a Slack message, email, or Google Doc that the team can asynchronously collaborate on?

Then gain express permission from everyone you intend on inviting. **Do not** send people random meeting invites. Conflict-avoidant people will just show up at your meeting (rather than decline the invite) and silently resent you for wasting precious hours of their lives.

Definitely do not send out an invite to a meeting you are not attending.

A good meeting invite must:

- Invite precisely the right people. When in doubt, mark people as "optional." Inexperienced managers will tend to over-invite people to meetings in an effort to make people feel included. There are better ways of achieving that.

- Clarify what kind of meeting this is (e.g., staff meeting, decision-making meeting, etc.).

- Have a comprehensive description that details the purpose of the meeting, expected outcomes, and the meeting owner who will run the proceedings. This should include a meeting agenda, with time allotted to the various discussion topics.

- Include a link to a shared Google doc or Asana project that everyone will be working out of.

- Be the right length. Meetings are often too long or too short, leaving dead space throughout the day that isn't long enough for focused IC work.

- Include a Zoom link; this is just common courtesy to remote folks.

One way to decide who the right people are is to identify how a person will contribute to the meeting. There are three ways in which participants can contribute to a meeting: 1) input, 2) decision, 3) commitment. If a person cannot make any of these three contributions, don't invite the person because this person just needs to be informed by broadcasting the meeting notes.

If you receive a meeting invite or request

Don't be afraid to decline meetings or request for their duration to be shortened. If you think the topic could be better handled in another format (e.g., asynchronously via Google Doc comments), then suggest it.

Decision meetings

Decision-making meetings are one-off events designed to gather information and key stakeholders in one place to—you guessed it—make a decision.

Most decisions will not need meetings. They can either happen asynchronously in an *issue and proposed solution document* or in staff meetings. Every now and again, a decision big enough will crop up to warrant its own meeting.

Just because you are meeting in person does not excuse preparation! Every decision-making meeting should include an issue or proposed-solution document linked to in the calendar invite.

The meeting should start with the owner assigning a note taker and then distributing the prepared document. Everyone reads it in silence to get in sync. Then the document is discussed and commented on.

There are two outcomes of a decision-making meeting. Either a decision is made, or it is noted that more information is required to make the decision.

Any next-actions made should be impeccable agreements. That means they are recorded in Asana, have an owner, a due date, and a good description.

Once the meeting is over, the meeting owner should distribute the notes to the relevant places, such as appended to the issue document and posted in team Slack channels.

Staff meetings

Staff meetings are recurring meetings for status updates, decision making, and action assignments. They are generally related to collaboration within a team, or between teams.

Staff meetings easily derail because they don't have a clear goal. Therefore, it's important for these meetings to have an owner who is ruthlessly managing them.

Every recurring meeting must have a corresponding Asana project that it is run out of. The format looks like this:

- ▾ Library
  - ⊘ Zoom Recordings   Ashley Hig...
  - ⊘ Notes 2 ○
- ▾ Updates
  - ⊘ GTM update   am amit
  - ⊘ Product update
  - ⊘ Goals & Stats
- ▾ Issues + Proposed Solutions
- ▾ Discussion Topics
- ▾ New Action Items
  - ⊘ Create standardized X qualification questions   Andrew O'...   Oct 31

Updates

Every key stakeholder must prepare an update prior to the meeting.

At the start of the meeting, everyone silently reads the updates. This is a huge amount of information transfer in the first ten minutes of the meeting, and it ensures that everyone is on the same page.

Issues (+ proposed solutions)

Prior to the meeting, issues are created. Each issue must have an owner, a good description, and ideally a proposed solution. If this is too long for an Asana comment, link to an external Google Doc.

Time-box each issue, and use a timer to ensure that you spend no more than five minutes per issue (Google "three-minute timer"). The idea is to get issues out of the way to spend more time on free-form discussion.

Discussion topics

These are general topics of discussion that aren't necessarily actionable. We find having some open-ended topics to be the most fruitful strategy when it comes to coming up with new ideas.

Examples of these might be a pre-mortem around an upcoming launch, a discussion on how to avoid partner channel conflicts, or debugging a team's performance issues.

Next actions

Any work to be done must be recorded in Asana; otherwise, it'll just be lost. We use Impeccable agreements for this. Every task must have an owner, a due date, and a good description.

The worst reason for a meeting

Most meetings are created in good faith by people who believe they are acting in the best interest of the company. Unfortunately, this is not always the case.

If your company starts rewarding people on relationships rather than outcomes, you will start building a toxic culture where junior people book meetings with senior people just to get "face time" and advance their careers.

The simple solution to this is *not* to reward "face time,". Cancel meetings you think were created for this purpose. The only way to get promoted is via our objective leveling system, not who you suck up to.

 Decision making

Writing vs. talking

Matt Mochary, in *The Great CEO Within*, has excellent advice on writing vs talking during decision making. We have reprinted it in full below.

When two people are discussing an issue, the need to be efficient is important. When a team is discussing an issue, the need to be efficient is paramount, because each inefficient minute is multiplied by the number of people in the discussion.

If you want the most effective and efficient decision-making process, **require that anyone who wants to discuss an issue write it up, along with the desired solution, ahead of time.** The goal of this write-up is to be thorough enough that at the time of the decision meeting, there are few or no questions. This can be achieved in one of two ways:

1. The hard way: Write an extraordinarily thorough analysis from the get-go.

2. The easy way: Write a draft, circulate it to the meeting participants before the meeting, and invite comments and questions. Then write out responses to all of these comments and questions prior to the meeting.

Jeff Bezos, founder and CEO of Amazon, is famous for using this written method. He requires that anyone who wants to bring up an issue or proposal must write up the item fully prior to the decision meeting (with someone else writing up a counterproposal if necessary). The meeting is then spent reading the write-ups. Once the decision-making team has read them all, a decision is made. If consensus is not reached, an appointed decision maker makes the call. If there are still open questions, then the decision maker assigns one or more people to research and, of course, write the needed follow-up. At the end of the next meeting, the decision is made.

This method, although time-consuming for the sponsor, yields extraordinarily thoughtful decisions in a very short amount of time. The extra effort and work by one person creates net savings in time and energy across the whole group.

Imposing this process on a group is daunting. Here is a way to ease a group into it.

1. Reserve the first 15 minutes of the meeting for all participants to write out their updates and issues. Then use another 10 minutes of the meeting for all participants to read each other's updates and issues. Then discuss and decide. Use this method for 2–3 meetings, then ...

2. Require that all participants write their updates and issues prior to the meeting. Do not allow people to bring up an issue that they have not already written up. Use the first 10 minutes of the meeting for all participants to read each other's updates and issues. Use this method for 1–2 meetings, then ...

3. Require that all participants write their updates and issues by a certain time prior to the meeting (e.g., 6 p.m. the evening before). Require that all participants read and comment on each other's updates and issues prior to the meeting. People can prove that they have read the docs by adding their comments in the docs themselves. Do not allow people to make comments in the meeting if they haven't already commented on the docs themselves. This will make your meetings much more efficient and ensure that meeting time is spent effectively.

Type 1 vs. Type 2 decisions

In his iconic 2015 Shareholder Letter [*bit.ly/shareholder15*], Amazon's Jeff Bezos introduced us to lightweight, distributed decision making. He wrote:

"Some decisions are consequential and irreversible or nearly irreversible—one-way doors—and these decisions must be made methodically, carefully, slowly, with great deliberation and consultation. If you walk through and don't like what you see on the other side, you can't get back to where you were before. We can call these Type 1 decisions. But most decisions aren't like that—they are changeable, reversible—they're two-way doors. If you've made a suboptimal Type 2 decision, you don't have to live with the consequences for that long. You can reopen the door and go back through. Type 2 decisions can and should be made quickly by high judgment individuals or small groups.

"Each time there is a decision to be made, rate it as Type 1 or Type 2. If Type 2, allow one of your reports to be the decision maker. The decision will be made faster, your report will get the chance to exercise their decision-making muscles, and you will have the chance to gain confidence in your report's ability to make decisions well."

Getting buy-in

Matt Mochary, in *The Great CEO Within*, has excellent advice on getting buy-in. We have reprinted it in full below.

One of the core challenges in leadership is how to get your team to buy into a decision. It's often easy to make a decision, but it can be much harder to get your team to invest emotionally in that decision.

You create buy-in when you make people feel that they are part of the decision and that their input contributes to the final outcome. The more influence they feel they have on the outcome, the more they'll be invested in the final result.

Broadly, there are three ways to make a decision. Each has a different time requirement and creates a different level of buy-in. There are no free lunches here, unfortunately—the method that creates the most buy-in also takes the most time.

The methods are:

1. Manager makes the decision, announces it to the team, and answers questions. Pro: Takes very little time. Cons: Creates very little buy-in from the team. Gets no benefit from their collective knowledge and experience.

2. Manager creates (or assigns someone to create) a written straw man (a hypothetical answer designed to inspire discussion), shares it with the team, invites the team to give feedback (written and verbal), facilitates group discussion, and determines the final answer. Pros: Creates more buy-in. Gets some small benefit from the collective wisdom of the team. Con: Takes more time.

3. Manager invites the team to a meeting where the dilemma is discussed from scratch with no straw man. Manager and team equally share ideas. Final decision is determined by consensus if possible. Pros: Creates the most buy-in. Gets a lot of benefit from the collective wisdom of the team. Con: Takes the most time.

Not surprisingly, the greatest benefits require the most work. If you want more buy-in and a better decision, you need to take more time in making the decision.

So, which method should you use? It depends on how significant the decision is and how important buy-in is. For everyday, low-impact issues (e.g., the venue for the holiday party), Method 1 is sufficient. For major, core issues (e.g., the company's 10-Year Vision), Method 3 is necessary. For everything in between (the vast majority of important decisions), Method 2 is optimal.

Disagree and commit

The dark side of consensus is that it can lead to inaction. "Disagree and commit" is a method of avoiding this trap. Jeff Bezos describes how he uses this at Amazon:

"Use the phrase 'disagree and commit.' This phrase will save a lot of time. If you have conviction on a particular direction even though there's no consensus, it's helpful to say, 'Look, I know we disagree on this but will you gamble with me on it? Disagree and commit?' By the time you're at this point, no one can know the answer for sure, and you'll probably get a quick yes.

This isn't one way. If you're the boss, you should do this too. I disagree and commit all the time. We recently greenlit a particular Amazon Studios original. I told the team my view: debatable whether it would be interesting enough, complicated to produce, the business terms aren't that good, and we have lots of other opportunities. They had a completely different opinion and wanted to go ahead. I wrote back right away with 'I disagree and commit and hope it becomes the most watched thing we've ever made.' Consider how much slower this decision cycle would have been if the team had actually had to convince me rather than simply get my commitment.

Note what this example is not: it's not me thinking to myself 'well, these guys are wrong and missing the point, but this isn't worth me chasing.' It's a genuine disagreement of opinion, a candid expression of my view, a chance for the team to weigh my view, and a quick, sincere commitment to go their way. And given that this team has already brought home 11 Emmys, 6 Golden Globes, and 3 Oscars, I'm just glad they let me in the room at all!"
— *Jeff Bezos, Amazon CEO*

🏝 Remote teams

Look around you and you will see distributed teams popping up everywhere. Companies like Zapier, Invision, and GitLab have paved the way, proving that it's entirely possible to build a thousand-plus team that is completely distributed. However, while remote teams have their advantages, they also come with their own challenges. It's important to go in with your eyes wide open, tackling these head-on.

Our team is 40% remote, with people living across the US, Europe, and even as far away as Israel. The rest of us are in San Francisco. We are a distributed company, rather than a remote one. The difference is that in a distributed company, you combine a central hub with remote employees, whereas a remote company is entirely virtual with no office. This structure can pose even more challenges than distributed companies, so it's important that we put a real effort into making our remote colleagues feel supported and included.

Why did we make the decision to hire remotely? Well, remote working offers some distinct advantages. First, it lets us hire the best people in the world—we're no longer limited to San Francisco's great but limited talent pool. Second, the flexibility it offers allows us to live richer lives. No longer are we limited to a 9–5 schedule, worried about making the school run, or fitting in that mid-day gym session.

 "Prior to working at Clearbit, Rob, one of our co-founders, had a two-hour commute to London every day and back. Not only was this exhausting, but he barely got to see his two daughters. Today, he works from home and gets to spend the rest of his time with his family. That extra time is priceless."

— *Alex MacCaw*

You might ask yourself, if remote working is such a great thing, why haven't companies offered it in the past? For starters, the technology wasn't there. Only in the last few years has video conferencing gotten to a level where it's fairly seamless and remote collaboration tools have become effective (e.g., Slack, Google Docs).

The other reason (which accounts for why most companies don't do it today) is control. Most companies are scared of losing control by offering their employees the flexibility of working from home. They're worried that the work isn't going to get done.

Our response to that is, who cares about controlling people? We treat people like adults by setting mutual goals and letting *you* decide how to hit them.

Remote working also changes how we do planning, decision making, and hiring. We will explore how we go about solving for these next.

The issues with remote

While the benefits clearly outweigh the costs, remote working does come with its own set of challenges. Most of these are deeply rooted in the human psyche. For example, we are hardwired to trust people we meet in person more than relative strangers. Video conference technology (in its current form) hasn't yet advanced enough to trick our monkey brains into thinking we're in the same room. We have so much nonverbal communication that the fidelity of conference just doesn't convey.

Latency is an issue too. If half a meeting joins from a room in San Francisco and the other half joins remotely, it's hard for people dialing in to interject themselves into flowing conversations.

Spontaneous conversations don't generally happen with remote teams. Whenever you call someone, it's for a specific meeting or request, not to ask them how their day went or to play with their dog. Again, this leads back to trust. To trust someone's intentions, you have to believe they have your best interests at heart. It's hard to do that without spending some quality time together.

We are social creatures. Working long hours, never leaving the house and rarely interacting with others, is a recipe for loneliness. Since there's no clear distinction between when your workday starts and ends, it can be difficult to set boundaries. We have heard from our remote team that their work tends to spill into their personal life.

So there's a combination of trust issues, practical collaboration issues, and lastly, loneliness. Some of these things can be solved with internal company policies, while others are up to the individual to manage. Before we discuss our approach to solving these issues, let's focus on the fundamentals: hiring people who like working remotely.

Hiring for remote

It's key that we identify and hire people that are happy working remotely. Even if we have the dopest office in San Francisco, in and of itself, an office can be a growth *limiter*. In order for Clearbit to scale successfully, we need to be a remote company that happens to have the dopest office in San Francisco.

The simplest hack is to hire people who've done remote work before. Quite frankly, the tradeoffs in remote work aren't for everyone. Remote work requires discipline, not only in actually sitting down and focusing, but also in taking the time for yourself to go outside and socialize. If someone has demonstrated they've been happy doing this in the past, we can assume they'll be happy doing it in the future.

If we do a good job hiring by our company values, then most folks are going to be successful in our organization, even if there is some turbulence along the way. When team members operate according to our values, they are force multipliers. Teams with common values have lower barriers for trust, they get along better with each other, and they align toward common goals more easily. Our people need to live and breathe **Team, Care, Craft, Truth, Initiative** and **Fun**.

Helpful interview questions

Tell me about your experience working outside of an office.

If they have no remote experience, it's not a deal-breaker, but it's much easier to bring in total newbs if we have a strong remote culture. If we haven't developed that yet, consider remote folks with more experience doing that so that they can help us build it.

What's your favorite remote working hack?

This is the organic part. We want to identify people who will be active participants in our remote culture and will bring great ideas to our organization. We want to avoid candidates who have a high risk of groupthink and social loafing.

Tell me about the space where you will be working.

If they don't have at least an idea of where they will be working, there will be other things they'll be clueless about. During remote interviews, take note of the candidates' location or office space. If it looks like it is a dedicated space and well put together, +1.

Have you worked on teams that spanned time zones? If so, how did you overcome those challenges?

Having to wait three hours to get a response from a West Coast team member sucks, but it's how the earth works. We want candidates that have initiative and manage their day and their work in a self-directed manner.

How do you initiate collaboration remotely? How do you force yourself to think outside your own perspective?

Candidates have to be self-starters and proactive in developing relationships with each other. If you think you will have to spend extra time and effort to get a remote candidate to interact with the greater organization, that's time and effort you will be taking away from your other top goals.

What company culture ideas would you like to bring over from your previous roles?

Can you buy in? Do you want to help us build a better machine? What does that machine look like to *you?* Can you say nice things about your previous companies?

Onboarding

Have a great 30/60/90-day plan

If you can't tell someone what you expect out of them in their first 90 days, you shouldn't hire them. If we hire to our values and we can clearly articulate a new hire's role and our definition of success, it makes their initial experience with Clearbit great. If we can't do that, then problems can be amplified when working remotely (i.e., paranoia that you aren't doing a good job, you don't want to ask dumb questions, misalignment on goals, etc.).

Fly them into the office for the first week

You want your team to develop trust and buy into the common company vision as quickly as possible. If remote teammates don't buy into the culture, company, and mission, they will churn. Without buy-in, working remotely for us becomes just like working for anyone else. We need them to fall in love with Clearbit, and we should give them a reason to. This is why we bring all remotes on-site for their first 1–2 weeks so they get a heavy dose of the Clearbit hotness to start them off right.

Pair them with a buddy for the first 90 days

The worst thing you can do for a new remote employee is to make them feel like they are alone. You should pair new hires with someone on their team for the first 90 days. Be deliberate who you pair together; ensure that they have enough time to dedicate to your new hire.

Make sure you do plenty of check-ins, and encourage folks on your team and other teams to reach out to new hires and welcome them to Clearbit. All new hires should have casual one-on-one hangouts within their first month.

Managing remote teams

Meet physically at least four times a year

It's just not possible to get around in-person meetings; our brains just aren't wired that way. Humans still struggle to trust each other without hanging out together and having some shared experiences. Even the most effective distributed companies still make a point to get everyone together once a year.

Think of having in-person interactions as charging a battery. Working from home slowly drains the battery, while visiting your team replenishes it. It's possible to get work done with a depleted battery, but it's less efficient. A good rule of thumb is that you need that battery recharged at least four times a year.

Team off-sites, company off-sites, and visits to our office in San Francisco are all great ways to recharge that battery and build trust between people. Humans bond over shared experiences, especially overcoming some type of adversary together. As a manager, you should be making space for these experiences with your team.

Clearbit will pay for the travel and accommodation costs of anyone visiting the office and will cover four such trips a year. We also have annual company and team off-sites.

Donuts

One of the issues working remotely is missing the random social interactions and "water-cooler chat" that can often spark new ideas or, at the very least, introduce you to people in the company you would otherwise not have much interaction with.

We use the Slack Donut [*donut.com*] bot to simulate this for remote workers. Every two weeks, this bot randomly pairs two people together, encouraging them to either hang out in person or over a Zoom call. These aren't structured conversations, so feel free to talk about whatever you'd like.

It's highly encouraged that everyone signs up, as we've found it to be a really effective way of building trust and helping our remote team feel included.

Games

We're hardwired from birth to play games. They're an integral part of the human condition. Observe any two children left to their own devices; their imagination lights up and the games begin.

As we grow into adults, it can be easy to dismiss games as childish, but they're an important part of bonding and trust building.

Some of our best remote teams play games together weekly. These can be anything from simple word-play games to Mario Kart on the Nintendo Switch. We also organize a monthly whole company Counterstrike "LAN" party.

Meeting etiquette

It's easy to feel excluded in a meeting when you're dialing in and all the other participants are physically in the same room. Speed-of-light limitations mean that you're always going to be at a latency disadvantage. When the conversation is flowing, it can be hard to get a word in edgewise.

There is a simple solution to this: if anyone attending a meeting is remote, then *everyone* is remote. It can feel silly dialing into the same Zoom call as the person in the adjacent call box, but it's an important part of remote collaboration.

We have found that, due to the size constraints of our office, sometimes there aren't enough call booths to have everyone join remotely. In this case, the meeting owner becomes the *remote advocate*, responsible for prompting remote attendees to give their opinion throughout the meeting.

Manage time zones

Remote is hard to pull off successfully as it is, but having people in widely disparate time zones makes things even more difficult! The worst is when someone is in a time zone all by themselves with nobody to chat with.

It's important to consider time zones when hiring and try to cluster people into similar time zones so they have some interaction. If you have to hire someone in a *really* remote time zone, make sure you are prepared to go the extra mile in making them feel included.

Have plenty of video touchpoints

Trust is a key indicator of success within remote organizations, but it's almost impossible to develop real trust with any other person if you never see them. Master efficient daily video stand-ups. Adopt talking over typing [bit.ly/talkingtyping] for simple asks. Promote the use of video collaboration across your team. If done correctly, your team should be able to name details of their teammates' remote locations (i.e., art on the office wall, books, etc.). It's those kinds of details that endear us to each other and foster trust.

 "Let's remember that pairing isn't just for engineers. One of my favorite things to do is spend 30–60 minutes with someone on my team just helping each other work on whatever is currently on their Asana tasks list. We come up with some of our best ideas this way. So if you're remote and feeling isolated, try

asking a few coworkers to schedule a 30–60 minute working
session every two weeks."

— Matt Sornson, Clearbit

The love has to be organic

You can't force culture on any group of people. The team dynamic needs
to be organic. Encourage members to team up to take on projects or
tasks and bring innovation to the team. Try to arrange trips or situations
where the team can meet and socialize in person. You can usually tell the
happiness of a team by the number of inside jokes they can tell.

Working remotely

Develop a routine

Working remotely can't be a big free-for-all. We find the best results
come from working within an established routine. For example, here's
one of our engineering lead's morning work framework:

 "My morning routine typically looks like this:

- Take 15 mins to plan out top goals for the day

- Work on the hardest thing(s) on the list for 2 hours

- Take a break and walk the dogs for 30 mins. If I'm blocked,
  I'm usually thinking of solutions

- Re-group list and work for another hour before lunch"

— Jason Dodds, Engineer at Clearbit

There will be different routines that work better for others, but overall, you should look to balance the freedom you get with remote work with the rigor of a daily framework of execution.

Be *you* everywhere, with your camera *on*

Always have your camera on for meetings and touchpoints. Please ask others to do so as well. This is non-negotiable. There should be no state in which you are working where your camera can't be turned on. If you look like ass, own the fact that you look like ass and understand that at some point the people you are talking to will look like ass too. If you don't want to turn the camera on because you are sitting in bed and it's all messed up, then get out of the bed and go sit at a table or something. This isn't rocket science. Be 100% of yourself at all times, but be professional.

Just because it is your home doesn't mean it's not your office

When you work at the office, you probably have a desk and chair and a dope monitor and all this good stuff to work with. You should have all that at home too. Make a point to have a dedicated place where you can work in peace. That place is not your bed. Know that you will be on video calls and that your surroundings need to be presentable. Be able to take a call without kids, roommates, or animals starting something in the background. We have a generous headphone allowance. Use it. You should be able to always have your mic on during a meeting. Don't be a Mutey Marvin.

Be available, but know when to turn it off

Develop a set of working hours during which your team members know they can count on you being available and communicate those hours with your team. Time zone deltas can make it extremely difficult for teams to collaborate, so make sure all team members are cognizant of their geographical differences.

When you're heads down trying to focus, set your Slack status to *away*. You can also use Slack's Google Calendar integration to automatically set your status when you're in a meeting.

Within your communicated hours, when a team member pings you on Slack, please respond as expediently as possible. Treat the request as if they are standing next to you. Conversely, you have to be very aware to turn your job off when it's time. It's really easy to jump back into work if you like doing it and it is always available. This can be a major source of friction with families and significant others. Make sure you disconnect during off-hours; most tools allow you to set this clearly, such as status in Slack, office hours in Google Calendar, etc. Please learn to use them, and use them effectively.

Lastly, take responsibility

Clearbit isn't responsible for our happiness. Nobody aside from you can take responsibility for that. Clearbit's commitment is to be a vehicle for our own self-growth. That means giving us the space, materials, and safety we need to grow. The rest is on us.

If your meetings aren't working for you remotely, take charge. For example, say, "hey guys, for our next team meeting can we try having everyone join via Zoom from their desks?"

If you're lonely, get a co-working space (we cover it) and be social with humans. Ask for help from your team (they love you and will jump at the chance to help).

If you feel like you're overworked and working until all hours of the night for people in other time zones, fix it. Set boundaries or change your working hours (if that fits your lifestyle). Being remote can be hard, but we're all here to support you in whatever you need to make it the best working experience possible.

Measuring managers' performance

If you have a goal you're working toward, the most effective way of making progress is to measure that goal and track your progress over time. When it comes to something as amorphous as management, though, how do you quantify it?

It turns out that you can track the level of employee engagement with 12 questions, and these questions work across any company and any industry. These questions are called the Gallup 12 [*bit.ly/gallupq12*], created by the same company that does election polling, and have been tried and tested across thousands of businesses.

Now, are the results of this survey directly correlated with managers' performance? No, there are lots of other variables (like the output of their team) that are very important to a manager's performance. That said, employee engagement is directly related to retention and productivity. Determining engagement across your team is a great way of seeing areas where you could improve.

The 12 questions are split into two parts, the first (esteem-needs) being the most important. Each question is scored 1 to 5, from *strongly disagree* to *strongly agree*, respectively.

The esteem-needs questions

1. Do I know what's expected of me at work?

2. Do I have the materials and equipment I need to do my work right?

3. Do I have the opportunity to do what I do best every day?

4. In the last week, have you received recognition or praise for doing good work?

5. Does my supervisor or someone at work care about me as a person?

6. Is there someone at work who encourages my development?

The self-actualization questions

1. At work, do my opinions seem to count?

2. Does the mission or purpose of the company make me feel like my job is important?

3. Are my coworkers committed to doing quality work?

4. Do I have a best friend at work?

5. In the last six months, has someone talked to me about my progress?

6. This last year, have I had the opportunity at work to learn and grow?

How we survey

We ask everyone in the company to fill out an anonymous survey to provide answers to the above questions twice a year. Then we share the raw, anonymized results with each manager and discuss areas of improvement. Note that for smaller teams, anonymity is hard to accomplish.

Below is an example of a table pivoted off each manager. The score represents the mean result across their reports.

	A	◀ ▶	C	D	E	F	G
▲ 1	Who is your manager?		Do I know what's	Do I have the me	Do I have the op	In the last 7 days	Does my supervi
▼ 3	Jennie Jolliff		4.80	4.60	4.25	4.40	5.00
4	Elisabeth Engelbrecht		4.33	4.33	4.33	4.67	4.67
5	Eulah Emily		4.50	4.50	4.00	4.75	5.00
6	Flo Futrell		4.00	5.00	4.00	5.00	5.00
7	Lenita Laux		5.00	5.00	5.00	5.00	5.00
8	Rosaura Rota		5.00	4.00	4.00	5.00	5.00
9	Catheryn Coad		4.75	4.50	3.75	3.75	4.50
10	Elmira Edberg		4.75	4.88	4.38	4.13	4.50
11	Tesha Tung		5.00	5.00	4.50	4.50	4.50
12	Saturnina Sweeney		3.00	3.50	3.00	5.00	3.00
13	Maya Machnik		5.00	4.00	4.00	5.00	5.00
14	Melodi Michaux		4.20	4.60	3.80	3.80	3.80
15	Blanca Baskerville		4.00	4.50	4.50	4.00	5.00

What to do with the results

An effective way of understanding how to improve the scores is to reverse the questions.

Esteem-needs questions reversed

1. Do my team members have clear job descriptions and clarity around projects, tasks, and expectations?

2. Does your team have the resources they need to succeed in their roles?

3. Do you have the right people in the right jobs, where they can use and build their strengths? Learn what people do best, and how their passions are different.

4. When was the last time you gave praise to the individuals on your team? If it wasn't in the last week, it's not regular enough. People crave recognition—your role as a manager is to encourage and cheer-lead your team.

5. Do you know who your team members are as people, not as employees?

6. Do you provide opportunities for your team to learn new skills and feel like they are moving forward?

Self-actualization questions reversed

1. What structure do you have in place for your team members to provide their feedback? Do you listen when it's given?

2. Do your team members know how their role fits into the bigger picture?

3. Are you letting poor performers set the standard, or are you encouraging people to lift the bar? Good performers can be demoralized if poor standards are accepted by others.

4. Are you providing opportunities for your team to grow supportive relationships at work? Work is a big part of their lives, so it's vital for people to have fun and friendship.

5. Are you providing regular reviews and feedback to help people with a sense of direction at work?

6. Are you providing opportunities for advancement?

How to improve

The most useful tool in your management arsenal is a one-on-one. Ask yourself the questions above, and then see how you can provide the support your team needs during their one-on-ones.

Are you setting clear expectations? Are you giving effective positive and critical feedback (see Feedback)? Are you discussing wider career growth opportunities with your team and providing a clear path to advancement? Most importantly, have you really gotten to know your team on a deep and personal level?

5. CREATING & ACHIEVING GOALS

 Clarity

In the early days of Clearbit, if you wanted to know what anyone was working on, you could just lean right over and ask them. Even at 50-ish employees, we did all-hands updates from every department. Now, at 100 people, it's now impossible for one person to know what everyone is working on. It's just too much information.

We asked Kenny Van Zant, one of our angel investors, about how to improve internal communication. He said, "I think you mean planning. Communication and planning are interchangeable." In other words, plan well and you will communicate well.

None of us need to know what every individual is working on. Knowing at least what every department's priorities are, though, is a key part of having clarity. If people don't have true clarity around what they're doing and how it fits into their organization, they're bound to duplicate efforts, deflate morale, spend hours on unimportant tasks, and more.

There's an excellent article on this in The First Round Review [*bit.ly/ JRstartup*]. To quote the pertinent parts:

 "When people don't know the order of operations, you get confusion, tension, drama. People get territorial because someone is already doing what they think they should be doing. And all you see are emails and meetings asking the same question over and over, 'What are you working on this week?'

When the details of projects, including who is responsible for what, exists outside a manager's head, and you make all this information available to everyone, you spread out accountability. It suddenly becomes very clear when someone has dropped the ball, or if someone doesn't have time to take on more work, or if more steps need to be taken before launch. Everyone is responsible for seeing and understanding the situation.

When management is freed up, they can focus their energy on more important things: Developing their people, providing important context around projects, upgrading tools. They're no longer spending all their time and energy simply serving as an information conduit. If your manager already knows what you're working on and the status of your work, you can use that meeting time that would otherwise be about what you did that week to talk about how you want to develop in your role, how you want to participate in the future of the company, etc. This is how great companies grow their futures."

— *Asana's Justin Rosenstein* on the One Quality Every Startup Needs to Survive [*bit.ly/JRstartup*]

There are six questions that everyone should be able to answer for them to have clarity:

- What are you working on right now?

- Are you confident that it's the most important thing you could be doing?

- Do you know who is waiting on you?

- Do you know who you can go to for support?

- Do you know how your work fits into the overarching product we're trying to create?

- Do you know why that product matters?

Or to summarize, clarity is composed of clarity of purpose, clarity of the plan, and clarity of responsibility.

The Pyramid of Clarity

It's no surprise that Asana (the company) dogfoods their own products and, being in the space they're in, they know a thing or two about planning.

Internally they use something called The Pyramid of Clarity [*bit.ly/ asanaclarity*] to ensure that everyone is aligned and working toward common goals. To quote them:

> The Pyramid of Clarity shows how our longer-term aspirations are built on top of shorter-term goals, whether we're building our product roadmap or business plans. We regularly refer back to the Pyramid of Clarity to help us stay on the same page, build confidence in our strategy and execution, and help individuals make decisions that are in line with the big picture.

The Pyramid of Clarity is a simple hierarchy of mission, strategies, objectives, and key-results. We prefer it over classical OKR systems because it's simpler (less hierarchy) and still manages to incorporate a larger mission.

This may seem like a lot of overhead, but you either pay the price of using this framework to consistently communicate (and how well you are performing) or you don't, and you have to respond on the backend to people who don't understand or get off track.

Mission

Great missions are short, clear, and could be stitched on a pillow. Things to remember about a good mission:

- Keep it high level. In general, a good mission tells someone who has never heard of your company not only what you do, but also *why you started the business.*

- A good litmus test is, if you tell your mission to a stranger, they can see why you're spending your life working on that.

- You want to tread the line between missions that are sufficiently broad and motivating, and those that are also specific enough. If you find yourself not referring to it a lot, it's not the right specificity.

Some good examples are:

* Asana: Enabling the world's teams to work together effortlessly

* Stripe: Increase the GDP of the internet

* Airbnb: Belong anywhere

* Google: Organize the world's information

* Nike: Bring inspiration and innovation to every athlete in the world

Strategies

If the mission is the "why" (inarguable because it's about passion), your strategies are "how" you will do it. At Asana, their strategy had three elements:

* Go build the best product in work management.

* Generate enough revenue to sustain the business and attract high quality stakeholders.

* Build the best team.

At Clearbit, we generally have four strategies for each year. In 2020 they were:

* Focus, focus, focus — on our ICP (less than 100K Alexa B2B companies)

* Deliver measurable impact for our ICP customers by building the next generation of marketing tools

* Be a "self-growth vehicle" for everyone on our team

* Continuously improve the unit economics (for our ICP) to build a business capable of growth in times of boom and bust

Objectives

At the tactical level, objectives are the tactical goal posts along the way toward accomplishing the strategies and ultimately the mission.

Here are some examples of our objectives over the years:

* Create a predictable product development process

* Create a relationship with all of our target accounts (Engagement, MQLs, Predicted Pipeline)

* Strengthen our culture of regular, candid bidirectional feedback

* Sustain a highly collaborative, inclusive, and remote-friendly culture

Objectives map to the strategies (and drive them). If you have big objectives that don't map to your strategies, it's a sign that your strategies should be tweaked.

Unlike classical OKR systems, we have a flat list of objectives and key results that don't inherit from one another. We have found that cascading OKRs don't work because it's confusing and results in sub-OKRs getting hidden and forgotten about.

Objectives should be realistically achievable within the year. There may be a lot of objectives (we have 10 top-level objectives this year). It's important that every objective is something the company should be doing, and that everyone's work contributes to at least one of them.

Objectives generally aren't quantifiable—that's the role of key results (covered next). We sometimes break this rule by having big revenue numbers in our objectives, but usually key results are what we are measuring against, not objectives.

Objectives are owned by an executive. They don't need to be restricted to a specific business area; they can have cross-functional boundaries or be company wide (one of the reasons they need to be executive owned).

The key is to be clear and simple. The organization of objectives gives everyone a framework to refer to—and it's also a communication framework, a roadmap to connect whatever you're working on all the way up to the mission.

If you find that parts of the organization are resisting negatively to the idea of objectives (or key results) in principle, rather than taking issue with a specific objective, that's a red flag. It's really important to identify those people early—many of them tap out because they don't like scrutiny on their prioritization or work.

Once your objectives are laid out, have multiple teams write key results against them.

Key results

Key results are measurements against your objectives to show how you're performing against them; for example, "generate $20M in new ARR." Every team will write key results against the various company objectives. They are refreshed quarterly.

Key results are:

1. Clearly defined

2. Owned by a single person (usually a team lead)

3. Objective, in that a third party should be able to confirm their current status

4. Ideally an integer value (rather than a true/false Boolean that has no concept of progress over time)

Whoever owns the key result should either have total control over the outcome (i.e., successfully achieving the key result doesn't hinge on teams that aren't reporting to them) or be an executive.

It's important that the team feels autonomy and agency over moving the key result. They shouldn't have to rely on other teams not under their control to achieve success.

That said, cross-functional objectives are often necessary. This is why we require cross-functional objectives to be owned by an executive who is often able to exert more influence over the organization and is more prepared to take ownership of things outside of their control.

One of the lessons we learned here is how to phrase KRs so others get a sense of progress. We use this format: From X to Y in *metric*. For example:

- From $10M to $20M in ARR

- From 10s to less than 1s in page load time

- From unknown to 40% 30d retention

Or written differently to achieve the same effect:

- Generate $20M ARR (up from $10M in q2)

We do it so that it communicates clearly how much velocity will be required to meet that goal and also whether there's a baseline available for it or not.

We suggest creating a Mode dashboard for each objective, listing out all the key results and their current value.

Initiatives

Lastly, initiatives are small projects that aim to drive progress against key results. They are small units of work at the single individual contributor level. They should be completely under the control of whoever owns them.

Recording OKRs

Our Pyramid of Clarity is stored in Asana. We use tasks for each objective. Key results are nestled under each objective as subtasks.

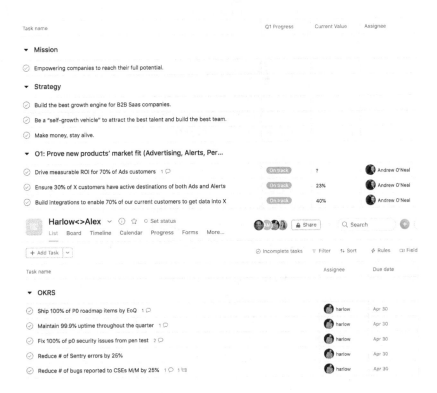

Updating Initiatives

For ICs that don't directly own a key result, their initiatives driving work toward the key result should be at the top of their one-on-one project.

Example of Q1 Initiatives at top of 1:1 board

🥇 Performance

The manager's dilemma is that they are responsible for the performance of their team but can't force anyone to perform.

It also seems odd that we would make someone responsible for something they can't control. However, that's not quite true; managers do have a degree of control over the output of their team. For a start, they get to pick the team (and make changes when required). They also help create the objectives and create a performance-conducive environment.

Why can't performance be forced? Well, this hasn't always been the case. Back in the industrial age, work in factories was mundane and repeatable. All performance required was putting in place a strict process and incentivizing people to follow it to a tee. In the information age, however, performance requires creativity, and creativity can't be coerced.

It turns out that creativity is especially difficult to cultivate; it requires a specific climate and careful nurturing.

Creativity is not an assembly line

Great managers set goals, not tasks. Giving a creative type too much direction is like overwatering your plants—it'll suffocate them. Your job is to communicate in detail the important challenges the company is facing and the immediate-term goals. Then ask your team to come up with proposals to achieve those goals.

Sure, those proposals might need a bit of editing, but by moving the decision-making process to your team, you are achieving two things:

1. Wisdom of the crowds. If you've hired well, your team should be making as good if not better decisions than you.

2. Buy-in. Great creative work is not achievable without your team's buy-in. An authoritarian approach only serves to dull the creative spirit.

Don't micromanage your team's work or daily output. If you find yourself supervising too often, you've hired the wrong people.

Setting goals

Good goal setting, especially at an individual level, is a learned skill. Goals should be:

- Audacious but achievable

- Clearly important (make sure your team understands *why* they are important)

- Aligned with your team's talents and individual goals

A great manager is able to describe the unique talents of each team member, and cast members into roles that play to these—just like a movie director.

We all have innate talents and strengths (see Zone of Genius), so don't try and change people. Instead, give them work they're going to be great at.

Ownership

Ownership is the key to performance. Think about how it feels when the company makes you responsible for a goal. Doesn't it feel exciting? Exhilarating? It's now up to you and your team to figure out how to achieve it. The rest of the company is trusting you. In short, you have agency.

Your job as a manager is to instill that feeling in the rest of your team. They should feel real autonomy and ownership over their work, and they should understand why it's important and how it fits into the greater picture.

Debugging poor performance

If someone is failing to achieve their goals (or getting anywhere close), then you have a performance issue. There is a simple thought experiment you can use for diagnosing this:

> "Ask yourself whether this person is capable of doing the work you want them to do if their life depended on it. Is it a question of motivation or a question of capability?
>
> If their life depended on it and they could do it, then that's on you as a leader not providing the proper motivation. Most of the time that's due to you not providing the larger story as to why their work is meaningful and the impact they will have.
>
> If however, they would be unable to do it even if their life depended on it, then that is your mistake as a manager for expecting them to be able to."
>
> — Lessons from Keith Rabois Essay 3: How to be an Effective Executive by Delian Asparouhov [*bit.ly/lessons-keith*]

Someone's ability to do a particular task is called "task-relevant maturity," which essentially means how much experience someone has in doing this task. We will cover this next in Delegation.

Manager myths

There are some common manager myths that keep them from capitalizing on their team's full potential. Try to avoid these myths!

* There's one best way (let your team figure out their best way).

* Certain roles don't require talent (everything does, to some degree).

* Trust must be earned (trust should be largely given by default—you've vetted your team thoroughly before they join).

* Some outcomes cannot be defined (a.k.a. the "I don't like my targets being measured" excuse).

 # Delegation

Delegation is the art of scaling yourself by distributing work across your team. The paradox of delegation is that it requires a degree of inefficiency and failure in the short term to work in the long term.

For example, let's say you have a task that needs doing. You look across your team, and decide that this work will only get done to your satisfaction if you're the one doing it. So you carve out some time to tackle it yourself.

At Clearbit, we call this heroing. Even if you're correct that you're the best person for the job, by not delegating, you're ensuring that your team never learns how to do this work, and subsequently your handling of this work can't be scaled.

For some work, this might make sense. For example, a CEO can't delegate a board meeting. However, you will find that most work can effectively be delegated. While initially it may not be done as well as you could have done it, the advantage of training your team and scaling yourself is worth it.

Task Relevant Maturity

So we've said before that great managers set goals, not tasks. However, what do you do in a case when someone has no experience in a particular area? Should you set a goal and leave them to sink or swim, or should you manage them closely by continuously asking for status reports and offering help? Task Relevant Maturity (TRM) answers this.

> "How often you monitor should not be based on what you believe your subordinate can do in general, but on his experience with a specific task and his prior performance with it – his task relevant maturity...as the subordinate's work improves over time, you should respond with a corresponding reduction in the intensity of the monitoring."
>
> — Andy Grove, High Output Management

So for reports that have no experience in an area (and therefore low TRM), then you need to be incredibly structured and closely manage their work. If they have done this task many times, then you can be far more laissez-faire and just check in occasionally. Managing this is a balance between micromanaging people's work and abdicating total responsibility.

Task Relevant Maturity

Low ←——————→ High

| Highly structured: | Set objectives and |
| What, when, how | lightly monitor |

As you can imagine, TRM is both very report – and task-specific. It is entirely possible for a person or a group of people to have a TRM that is high in one job but low in another. You want to raise a given person's TRM as fast as possible, to the point where you are setting mutually agreed-upon goals with occasional check-ins.

Delegating decision making

It's tempting to try and make all the decisions yourself. After all, you might have a lot of context and you might have been at the company longer than your team—surely you're going to make better decisions?

However, this gets into the management trap we discussed earlier. By not trusting your team, they will never learn to make decisions themselves, and you can never scale (or go on vacation).

By default you should be delegating decisions. Some decisions are too mundane for making the best use of your time (what coffee filters to buy), and some decisions are too specific and require domain knowledge you may not have. Know that anytime you make a decision (or override your team), you burn social capital with them; you're showing them you don't trust them.

Trust requires judgment, which requires trial and error. Delegating decisions, therefore, inherently involves a degree of inefficiency and failure. In most cases a certain level of failure is acceptable, but what do you do in cases where failure is catastrophic? There is a simple framework.

The trade-off is between your level of conviction (i.e., do you think you know the ideal right answer?) and the consequence (i.e., if you make the wrong decision, how catastrophic is the downside?).

Level of conviction		Consequence of decision	
		Low	High
High		Roam free	Step in. Decide. Overrule.
Low		Delegate fully	Gather more information

Here's how you should think about using the framework: when your conviction is low and the consequence low, delegate the project fully. When your conviction is high and the consequences low, delegate but monitor closely—it's better to extend the rope and let your report gain experience (and TRM). When the consequences are high, you either need to gather more data or overrule.

One way of understanding the consequence of a decision is determining whether that decision can be reversed or not. We call these Type 1 or Type 2 decisions, and we cover them in Decision making.

6. INFORMATION SHARING

🏛 Internal communication

The larger a company grows, the harder it is to make sure everyone has the information they need. As the company scales, more information is generated. At this point, it is impossible for any one person to hold the whole state of the company in their head.

There are a number of factors we need to consider when thinking through internal comms:

- The relative priority of pieces of information, and who needs to know what and when

- The synchronous or asynchronous nature of the communication channel (e.g. email vs. Slack)

- The efficiency of the human brain processing different types of communication (e.g. written vs. verbal)

- The purpose of the communication (knowledge transfer vs. behavior change)

- The remote nature of this company

Clearly not *all* information needs to be communicated *all* the time. We just need to make sure the right bits of information get to the right people over the right channels.

We also have to consider the purpose of some types of communication, some of which is not to transfer information, but rather to motivate (e.g., rah-rah speeches at an all-hands). While written communication is a more efficient medium than verbal, it's less motivational.

Lastly, when designing internal comms, we need to take into account the fact that people have different learning styles and information processing abilities.

Communication etiquette

It is important to use etiquette when picking a channel to communicate, especially when asking for help. Consider how urgent your message really is. Can it wait a day to get a response? Everyone has problems. What makes your problems more important than whatever someone is currently working on?

For example, one thing we see is a false sense of urgency given to sales deals or renewals that have suddenly become the company's "top priority." Time sensitivity is important, but the vast majority of things are not urgent. Just because you have a vested interest in a deal going through doesn't mean you can stomp over other people's priorities.

A good rule of thumb is to assume a **same-day response** unless the issue is actually urgent (e.g., the servers are down).

If you are on the receiving end of this "false urgency," it's totally fine to push back and ask exactly how urgent something really is and what will happen if it's delayed.

Distractions

Communication can be incredibly distracting. While some jobs require a lot of communication (e.g., sales), some require deep periods of uninterrupted thinking time (e.g., engineering). If your role looks more like the latter, then turn off all notifications and keep Slack closed when you need to concentrate. Set expectations with your manager and colleagues that you won't be available during certain hours, and to call you if something incredibly urgent comes up (e.g., the servers are down).

> GitLab uses a company-wide tool called Clockwise [*getclockwise.com*] that automatically stops Slack notifications during a defined "focus time." It also syncs calendars to alert others if the employee is in a meeting, whether it's an internal or external meeting, without having to check the calendar.

Storing information

Transferring information is different from storing information. We have a 30-day retention policy in Slack. This is intentional. We want to encourage you to copy any information that needs to be retained into our wiki.

Communication and tasks

Asking someone to do something over Slack is a good recipe to ensure that it doesn't get done. Slack makes a terrible task manager. You can hack it a little by using the "remind me about this message" feature, but ultimately tasks get lost in Slack.

It turns out that humanity invented a pretty good task manager in the 1970s called email. Gmail has built-in algorithmic prioritization, starring, and tagging features that make it half decent at holding tasks—certainly much more than Slack. Once you have an agreement with someone, make it impeccable by recording it in Asana.

Why not just skip emails and create tasks directly in Asana? Surely that would save time? There are two reasons:

1. Generally it is better to set goals rather than tasks. Creating a task for your report directly in Asana assumes you know the answer to your query; your report should be the judge of that.

2. Impeccable agreements have to be *mutually* agreed *upon because the owner is accountable.* Creating a task directly removes that option.

Why not skip tasks and just use emails? It's important that all tasks are in one place (Asana), have a due date, an owner, and be commonly accessible across the company. Only a shared task manager fulfills those criteria.

One exception to this is creating a task in Asana to serve as a topic for your next one-on-one; that's entirely fine.

Please adhere to the following table when picking your communication channel. It can be tempting to just direct-message (DM) someone on Slack in order to move past your issue quickly. That, however, results in the tragedy of the commons. While one DM is fairly harmless, if we all act this way, the company grinds to a halt.

Communication type	Communication medium
To an individual, asking them to do something	Email
To an individual about a complex private topic	Email
A question you need help with	Check the wiki first, then ask in the relevant team's Slack channel (avoid PMing)
To an individual about a topic that could be relevant to others	Slack Public Channel Message
To an individual about a private topic	Slack Private Message (PM)

Communication type	Communication medium
A daily update about your work	In your team's dedicated standup channel
Any communication with an external party	Email (BCC a list)
Communication about a task	In Asana on the task
Communication about code	In GitHub
An all-hands update about your department	In Slack's #all-hands channel
A full company update	In Slack's #general channel, and reiterated at all-hands
Communication that everyone absolutely needs to see	In the New Tab section in Contentful, in the #general channel, and then reiterated at all-hands.

External email communication

We ask that by default any external email communication is BCCed to a list. This allows anyone in the company to search their inbox for communication and get context for, say, a sales call. You can find a description of all these lists in our wiki under *Email Lists*.

Conference calls

We use Zoom for all video/audio conference calls. The quality is better than other tools we've used.

We use Chorus.ai to record all external calls. This transcribes the audio content and makes it searchable. It's a very useful tool for the team because it lets us see in aggregate how customers are reacting to products we develop, how often competitors are mentioned, and other data. It is also invaluable for onboarding new employees, who can learn from the calls.

We also use Zoom's "record call" functionality for internal meetings too, especially for recurring meetings. You'll notice that throughout our wiki we have links to Chorus/Zoom calls. We use this as a learning resource, to showcase great customer calls, and in case people need to catch up on meetings they missed.

Add "record@chorus.ai" to your calendar event to easily record an external meeting.

Slack communication

We use Slack for a lot of internal communication. Slack is a powerful tool, but it's easy to misuse.

* Avoid PMing (private messaging) people if possible. Ask someone a question in a public channel so others can learn from the answer.

* Check the wiki first before asking a question.

* Aggressively mute channels so that your unread messages count is accurate.

* Default to using threads for topics.

* We have a 30-day retention policy. Any information that needs to be retained beyond that should be in the wiki.

Name	Description
#shout-out	Say something good about someone (keep it specific)
#shipped	Sales/CS deal closed, or a big feature shipped

Name	Description
#eng-shipped	Something super-duper technical got shipped
#remote	All things remote with a 24hr Zoom Room
#random	Weird and random facts, off-topic binny discussions
#general	Announcement only
#all-hands	Links and other resource posted during all hands
#devops	Developer hangout
#sales	Sales team hangout
#customer-success	CS team hangout
#growth	Marketing team hangout
#data	Data team hangout
#data-support	Ask data questions
#it-help	Ask IT questions

Shipped

It's important that we celebrate shipping; it's part of our culture. Whenever anything gets shipped, and this could be a closed sales deal, a renewal, or a big feature it gets posted in the #shipped Slack channel. Don't be shy with the emojis!

Cross-sell/upsell bot APP 2:47 AM
Guess what? Customers love us so much that we landed a cross-sell/upsell! (view in Salesforce)

Opportunity: SFDC E 2020 - Early Renewal & Upsell
Reps: Will Frey and Margo Cleveland
Deal Team: Margo
Type: Renewal
Amount: $25,816.00
Baseline ARR: $16,800.00
Net New ARR: $10,416.00
Products: Early Renewal Credit, Enrichment- Salesforce
Contract Length: Annual
Billing Frequency: Annual

Company
Name:
Website:
Employee Count: 150.0
Alexa Rank: 76,860.0
Location: San Francisco, CA United States
Description: I

Notes
Use Case: Increase database limit in Salesforce
Business Outcome: Continue to enrich all leads
Key Features / Fields: job title, industry, employee count
Source: Existing Customer

👍 21   🔥 22   📝 9   😄

Meeting communication

We have a whole section on how to run a meeting (Running meetings), so refer to that regarding how to communicate in a meeting.

Transparency

For much of history, companies have tightly controlled the flow of information. There were many justifications for this, from concerns about secrets falling into the hands of competitors to the practice of using information as a form of compensation. The risks of transparency outweighed the potential benefits.

These incentives have all flipped in the information age. Modern tech companies consist of a small number of smart and leveraged people writing software to solve their problems. Creativity, rather than control, is now at the leading edge.

All of this lends itself well to a culture of transparency:

1. Transparency increases our creativity surface area. The more brains we have working on our hardest problems, the more likely we are to solve them.

2. Transparency builds mutual trust. Trust breeds creativity.

3. Because we don't have to manage the state of who knows what, a transparent culture improves the efficiency of communication, helping us collaborate better.

This is why we default to transparency in all cases (aside from cases related to compensation and performance, which are personal issues). To be clear, this doesn't mean everything is transparent, but we share as much as we can.

What transparency doesn't mean

When we first started out, we made the mistake of thinking transparency meant giving everyone a firehose of information. The sheer amount of information we shared ended up overwhelming people.

Transparency doesn't mean giving all the information all the time. It just means the information is available for anyone who wants to find it.

Mutual trust

Facebook and Google, two companies previously known for their corporate transparency, have started scaling back what they share internally.

Google even got rid of their town-hall style meeting held every Friday. What sparked this change? Leaks.

Trust is a two-way street. In order to have transparency, it's extremely important that information is kept confidential. Please don't share information like revenue numbers outside the company. It only takes one bad actor to spoil it for everyone.

Practicing what we preach

The most transparent thing we do as a company is publish our Leadership offsite notes. These include retrospectives of the quarter, 360 feedback, and a breakdown of how we're feeling emotionally.

These aren't the raw notes; we redact parts of them related to performance or compensation (if we didn't, it could become an exercise in public shaming).

Metrics transparency

Our ARR (annual recurring revenue) will always be shared with the company, so everyone has a good idea of the progress we're making. Additionally, we present high-level financials (P&L overview, cash in bank, etc.) every month to the company.

Meeting transparency

By default, internal meetings should be recorded in Chorus.ai. This lets anyone who didn't attend the meeting catch up on the contents, and is especially important for our remote teammates who operate in different time zones. We recommend putting a link to the Chorus recording into a relevant spot in the wiki.

Funding transparency

The amount of money we've raised, and the various valuations, can be found in our wiki.

Email transparency

By default, emails should be CCed or BCCed to an internal list. We follow Stripe's approach to email transparency [*stripe.com/blog/ email-transparency*]. Since most of our communication is over Slack (covered below), this will generally come into practice when communicating externally.

Email transparency helps spread context around deals, support issues, and customer requests around the company, and it helps us communicate internally and build a better company.

Slack transparency

Direct messages should be avoided in Slack. By default, you should be using a public channel. It's especially important for any questions to be posted publicly—the answers may help everyone on the team. There's a lot of institutional knowledge locked up with a few people, and this is a good way of spreading it.

If you get a question asked of you in a private channel, then politely bubble it up to a public channel so everyone can learn from your response.

Additionally, if a question is being asked multiple times, then it's time for a wiki article to be created.

We have channels set up for most areas of the business, but just post the message in the most appropriate channel you can find. Use Slack threads for any responses.

Documentation

We've gotten a lot of advice over the years in building Clearbit, much of it instrumental to our success. One such piece was given by Moisey Uretsky, cofounder of Digital Ocean, concerning documentation.

According to Moisey, documentation was the secret to how Digital Ocean effectively scaled up the company, letting them rapidly hire hundreds of employees without grinding to a halt. Not only did they document every process inside the company, but they made documentation a core part of their culture.

Why does documentation work so well? Let's consider the alternative: storing information in people's brains. Brains are meant for having ideas, not storing them. Brains have slow information retrieval (you have to interrupt someone), slow information transferral (verbal communication is much slower than written), and they also can't be searched.

As the company scales, the amount of questions that need to be answered on a given day also scales. If your team members are asking each other these questions, rather than referencing documentation and teaching themselves, scaling is impossible.

Scaling documentation

There are now over 6 million articles on Wikipedia. How did they manage to scale this up without sacrificing quality? Not through central planning, that's for sure. It is physically unfeasible for one person to plan or manage such a large amount of information. No, they scaled by distributing consensus among thousands of editors applying the same standards.

What worked for Wikipedia will work for us. That means we are *all* responsible for documentation. If you create a product or process, document it in our wiki. If you have a question, and the wiki doesn't already contain the answer, document it. If you're onboarding and notice some documentation is wrong, fix it. We all need to become editors.

I have a question

One of the most defining aspects of an organization is how it handles questions. A question is a failure of onboarding, since a perfect onboarding process would teach everyone everything (so they have no questions). However, since our onboarding will never be perfect, we need a system for handling questions when they invariably crop up.

The system goes like this:

1. You have a question.

2. First, search our wiki to see if it contains the answer.

3. If that doesn't work, search our API docs [*clearbit.com/docs*], attribute docs [*clearbit.com/attributes*], and help center [*help. clearbit.com*].

4. If that doesn't work, ask the question in a public Slack channel (the most appropriate teams).

5. Wait ten minutes.

6. If that doesn't work, look up the person who's directly responsible via the AOR sheet (Areas of responsibility), and private-message them on Slack.

7. Lastly, and this is the most important step, *record* the answer in the wiki so the next person who has this question doesn't have to go through the entire process again.

Documenting processes

Every single process at the company is documented in our wiki. From how to open the office on the weekend to how to run payroll to how to rollback a migration, it's all in there.

As we covered earlier, this is much more efficient than storing these processes in people's brains. This approach comes with another advantage, though: reducing our bus factor [*deviq.com/terms/bus-factor*].

The more information that's stored in people's heads, the more single points of failure we have. People aren't available for all sorts of reasons. They go on vacation, get sick, or leave the company. When they're unavailable, work gets blocked. We need to ensure that whatever is in their brains gets documented before that happens.

🚑 Areas of responsibility

The "tragedy of the commons" is that when several people share responsibility for an action or process, often that action doesn't get done well, or at all.

The phrase comes from a story about The Commons, a shared grazing area between farmers. When one farmer's flock grazes on the common land it reduces the quality of the land available for other farmers. Because people overlook this negative externality when deciding how many sheep to own, the result is an excessive number of sheep, and an un-grazable Common.

To prevent this from happening, we group tasks into categories and assign each category to one—and only one—person, the directly responsible individual (or DRI). These are our Areas of Responsibility (or AORs). Apple is famous for having pioneered AORs in Silicon Valley, but now most successful tech companies use this method.

We've created a listing of every possible function in the company. Next to each function, we list the responsible person. This is the AOR list. It serves as a company directory and ensures that no functions fall through the cracks. It should be updated as new functions arise or as responsibilities shift.

This, combined with our process documentation, ensures that there are no single points of failure.

Sample AORs

AOR	DRI	Backup	Slack Channel
Develop cross-product roadmap	Andrew O'Neal	AlexMacCaw	
Manage QA team	Wei Zhu	Ben Stevenson	
Product Design	Hector Simpson		
Manage designs and design approval	Andrew O'Neal		
Signoff on final products	Andrew O'Neal	Alex MacCaw	
Product Management: X	Ashley Higgins	Andrew O'Neal	#x-support
Product Management: API	Wei Zhu	Harlow Ward	#data
Product Management: Data	Wei Zhu	Harlow Ward	#data
Product Management: Connect	Jess Lam	Andrew O'Neal	#integrations-support
Product Management: HubSpot, Pardot, Marketo	Jess Lam	Andrew O'Neal	#integrations-support
Product Management: Salesforce	Jess Lam	Andrew O'Neal	#salesforce
Product Management: Pricing	Amit Vasudev		
Product Support: Shirley Shaw			#support
Webhooks	Ben Stevenson	Wei Zhu	#data

No single point of failure

A single point of failure is a function that one person performs when no one else has full knowledge of how that function works. If that person becomes sick or leaves the company, functionality suffers. A well-run company has no single point of failure. To create a team with no single points of failure, we do two things:

1. Write down all processes. As soon as you or your team members find yourselves doing something for the second time, you should write down the steps of that process exactly (so you don't have to explain the third time). Place these written processes in Notion.

2. Cross-train a second person for each role. Map each function in the company (from the AORs) to a backup person. Have the backup person co-work with the primary until the backup knows how to perform the role. (Of course, having all of the processes already written down will vastly improve this training process, so have your team write down all the processes first.)

7. CONFLICT RESOLUTION

😇 Good conflicts

Conflicts range from the extreme to the mundane, from the battlefield to the boardroom. And, while conflict generally carries a negative connotation, it's also (somewhat paradoxically) the engine powering our entire civilization.

The physicist David Deutsch puts it well:

> "The majority of human history has constituted as a long period of complete failure to make any progress. Our species has existed for 200,000 years. For the vast majority of that time, people were alive, they were thinking, they were suffering, they wanted things. But nothing ever improved. The improvements that did happen happened so slowly that geologists can't distinguish the difference between artifacts from one era to another with a resolution of 10,000 years. So from the point of view of a human lifetime, nothing ever improved, with generation upon generation upon generation of suffering and stasis.
>
> Then there was slow improvement, and then more-rapid improvement. Then there were several attempts to institutionalize a tradition of criticism, which I think is the key to rapid progress in the sense that we think of it: progress discernible

on the timescale of a human lifetime, and also error correction so that regression is less likely. That happened several times and failed every time except once—in the European Enlightenment of the 17th and 18th centuries."

In summary, every brick in the road of our civilization was laid by the process of critiquing ideas, trying to determine which make sense and which should be discarded. In periods where idea critiquing was either censored or otherwise not part of our culture, progress stalled.

Critiquing ideas naturally involves a degree of conflict. Ideally, conflict is resolved with words, but sadly, all too often throughout human history, it has been resolved with violence. It's no wonder most of us have a natural aversion to it.

Compounding this, our language doesn't even make a distinction between the good kind of conflicts (the ones that result in science and progress) and the bad kind of conflicts (the ones that result in violence and war).

Good vs. bad conflicts

Conflict is paradoxically one of the most destructive and constructive forces we have. Clearly we should try and harness the power behind the good kind of conflict and try to avoid the bad kind of conflict, but how do we differentiate between the two?

Certainly good conflicts are fought with words rather than violence, so that's a clear distinction. But you only have to open up Twitter to see the bad kind of conflicts fought with words, so clearly we need to look for further distinctions.

Another distinction is intent. The intent behind a productive conflict is to find the truth rather than to be right. Of course, determining intent is easier said than done. But if someone is displaying a distinct lack of curiosity that's a sign that they're not interested in the good kind of conflict.

Another distinction is outcome. Do both parties come away energized? Was progress made toward finding the truth? Or was the conflict personal, culminating with a gleeful winner and a dejected loser?

Outcomes are important because they teach us what to do in the future. If conflicting ideas are resolved amicably and all parties feel like progress toward truth was made, then the teaching is to embrace good conflicts. But if conflicts are heated, personal, or involve ad-hominem attacks, then they teach us to be conflict avoidant. And thus, to make less progress.

Conflict avoidance

Because the word *conflict* is such a catch-all in our language, both good and bad conflicts occupy much of the same thought processes and trigger the same emotional responses (freeze, fight or flight). The net result: we avoid all types of conflict, often to the detriment of making progress.

We all have different tolerances for conflict. It turns out that people with a higher tolerance for conflict tend to get further in life—particularly managers, whose performance is directly related to the number of difficult conversations they're prepared to have. That's not to say that you should love conflict for conflict's sake (those people tend to be assholes), but only that you shouldn't shy away from resolving important conflicting ideas in a search for the truth.

So how do we train ourselves to be less conflict avoidant? We can use the same technique that therapists use for treating phobias: systematic desensitization. That's basically a fancy way of saying "exposing yourself to something over time." In this case, we need to set up a culture where conflicts are consistently resolved productively.

How to ensure productive conflicts

A nice benefit of starting a company is you get to set the rules in your playground. And, as a manager, you too get to set the terms of engagement on your team. By getting a commitment up-front from them to follow general principles designed to encourage good conflicts, you can increase the chance that conflicts are resolved amicably and progress is made.

Rapoport's Rules, named after game theorist Anatol Rapoport [*bit.ly/rapoport-about*], are a set of rules intended to encourage productive, critical discourse. In particular, the rules seek to avoid straw man representations of an opponent's argument and to avoid the backfire effect that criticism often provokes.

The rules are as follows:

1. You should attempt to re-express your target's position so clearly, vividly, and fairly that your target says, "Thanks, I wish I'd thought of putting it that way."

2. You should list any points of agreement (especially if they are not matters of general or widespread agreement).

3. You should mention anything you have learned from your target.

4. Only then are you permitted to say so much as a word of rebuttal or criticism.

The reason that following Rapoport's Rules makes for a more productive conversation is that both parties feel *heard*. If you can state your opponents arguments as well as they can, they feel heard and will extend you the same courtesy.

We think these rules are a great start, but would humbly submit some additions:

1. Seek the truth rather than trying to be right; take the ego out of it.

2. Hold ideas lightly and keep your identity small [*paulgraham.com/identity*].

3. Speak in absolute truths (either with facts, or with personal truths like "I felt ...")

4. Remember, context over content. If someone "doesn't want to hear it," more words aren't going to help. Both parties need to be operating in a curious state.

In a marriage, it often helps to reframe conflicts away from "you vs. your spouse" to rather "you and your spouse vs. the problem." We think a similar reframing is useful in the office too. Starting with what you agree with, state your shared goals and then team up to find the best possible solution.

Remember, if someone changes your mind, that's a *good thing*. They've done you a favor by error-correcting your model of the world.

 "I don't mind being wrong. And I'll admit that I'm wrong a lot. It doesn't really matter to me too much. What matters to me is that we do the right thing."

— *Steve Jobs*

Learning through curiosity

Before giving someone feedback, debating through ideas, or really any kind of conversation, it's worth considering the *context* before the content. This means considering (and potentially addressing) everyone's emotional state before you're deep in a conversation.

If humans were logical calculating machines, then this wouldn't be a problem. Your iPhone doesn't care if it's at 10% battery, it's still going to compute accurately. Humans, on the other hand, are barely accurate at the best of times. And when we are tired, angry, sad, or scared, our higher-level thinking completely shuts down.

Thousands of years of evolution developed our *intuition*, a type of reflex thinking designed to improve our survival. It also baked cognitive biases [*bit.ly/biaseslist*] into us—a list that goes on for several pages. All this was well meaning. Biases are energy preservation hacks that were useful at some point on the savannah. But they struggle in dealing with modern life's complexity.

In our experience, the greatest bias of all is emotional state. When someone is angry, sad, or fearful, they tend to not make rational decisions or innovate. Instead they stall, attack, and avoid.

What compounds this is a rather strange sense of delusion that none of this exists. Because our sense of self is restricted to our unobjective reality, we get so wrapped up in our own world (and being right), that we assume these biases only apply to others.

So, in order to have productive conversations, first determine (and, if needed, address) the emotional state of the room.

Determining emotional state

Getting a grasp on how we're feeling at any given point in time is easier said than done. This is because, as we grow up, we're taught to hide our feelings from others. To be a good actor, you have to live the part, which involves a degree of hiding those same feelings from yourself as well.

We're not born this way, though. Toddlers, for instance, have no filter. If they're happy, they smile; if they're sad, they cry; if they're angry, they lash out. But as we grow up, society dulls these edges. And it's a good thing too—nobody wants a world run by toddlers.

However, reverse-engineering some of this programming is valuable. A key part of emotional maturity is pausing before reacting, locating yourself, understanding what you're feeling, and asking yourself if you're in a curious, open-minded state. And then, and only then, reacting.

It doesn't matter if you think feelings are useless. The fact of the matter is, you have them, and they affect your judgement. It's better to come to terms with that and incorporate them into your mental models than to live in denial.

Feelings manifest themselves in different ways in the body. Many people feel anger as a tightness in the chest. Or a flush in the face. Similarly fear often manifests as a chill across the skin. Staying attuned to these changes in your body can give you clues to your emotional state.

In others, you have to go by visual and audio cues. Humans are pretty good at that; indeed, we're often better at determining emotions in other people than in ourselves. But, when in doubt, ask.

Interpersonal conflicts

Of course, many conflicts in a company are not about ideas, but about people. These are harder to resolve because they're caused by fundamental distrust. Often interpersonal conflicts are masquerading as conflicts about ideas. It's important to realize this early and address the root cause—quibbling over ideas is just a front. We address this in the next section: Issue resolution.

> For further reading, we suggest this paper [*bit.ly/conflic-tres1994*] by Neil Katz and Kevin McNulty of the Department of Conflict Resolution Studies.

 Issue resolution

Issues are bound to crop up in the day-to-day running of a company. Rather than try and prevent them, instead focus on an effective issue-resolution system.

There are three types of issues:

1. Tactical (i.e., something is about to go wrong)

2. Performance-related (i.e., something went wrong)

3. Interpersonal (i.e., people not trusting each other)

Interpersonal issues are usually the most complex to deal with. People with interpersonal issues talk past and ultimately lose trust with one another.

Fortunately, we have developed good systems for resolving these different types of conflicts. Remember, the key to all conflict resolution is tackling it early; don't let things fester. And the key to tackling it early is regular, scheduled, bi-directional feedback.

Resolving tactical issues

Tactical issues are usually decisions hiding as issues. Team members will often want to bring up an issue and discuss it verbally. This is both inefficient (talking takes longer than reading) and ineffective (only the most forward people speak up and get heard).

Instead, require that anyone who presents an issue at a team meeting do so in writing. This should be in the *Issues and Proposed Solutions* section in the relevant meeting's Asana project.

The write-up should include both a detailed description of the Issue as well as their Proposed Solution. They may say "I don't know the answer," but they should take a guess. This may seem aggressive, but it creates a flag in the sand, which generates a much more productive discussion and a quicker decision time, which ultimately is more important than appearing to be humble.

Resolving performance issues

Performance issues happen when mistakes are made (e.g., an email newsletter sent to the wrong people). They are best addressed either immediately (in a private setting) or shortly after (in a one-on-one).

Usually these are quickly resolved. Once you've given the feedback regarding the mishap, we suggest asking for a "habit" to ensure that it doesn't happen again. For example, you could create a checklist to run through before, say, releasing a blog post.

Larger issues require a post-mortem to learn from them and prevent them from recurring in the future.

Resolving interpersonal issues

Interpersonal issues are generally caused by a lack of trust between two people—trust that someone understands what you're saying, trust that they will do a good job, or trust in their motives (are they acting in the best interests of the company).

Usually interpersonal issues happen because people don't feel heard by each other. There is a simple solution to this: repetition. Get both parties to say "what I heard was... is that right?" and summarize what the other said. It sounds too simple to work, but it does.

Deeper interpersonal issues require Clearing conversations. Don't let these conversations linger—they will just fester until resolution is impossible.

👌 Clearing conversations

When trust has broken down between people, it is time for a clearing conversation. This is a scripted and moderated dialogue between disconnected parties. Its purpose is to rebuild trust through listening, curiosity, and revealing stories.

Of course, it would be better to not get to this point. Clearing conversations are ultimately a process failure. It generally takes a while for trust to get this broken, with ample opportunities to fix it along the way.

How does trust fundamentally break down between people? Ultimately it's a combination of not feeling heard, withholding feedback, toxic story creation, and suspicion about each other's motivations.

What builds trust? Candid conversations where each side feels heard. Giving and receiving feedback. Overcoming shared adversity. Clearing up negative stories. Reaffirming shared goals and values.

A clearing conversation is a sign that some of those trust-building activities are not happening. Generally this manifests with feedback withholdings (e.g., one or both of the parties involved are afraid of giving each other feedback, or they've created a bunch of stories about each other that they're not clearing up).

But ... we're all human. Most of us are by default conflict avoidant, and even the best teams get into situations where people are at loggerheads. The good news is that *clearing conversations* are a tried and tested technique to resolve this. We've used them dozens of times at Clearbit to great effect.

Clearing conversation checklist

It is essential that you are willing to let go of being right and take responsibility before you attempt to use this model. If you haven't run one of these conversations before, ***make sure you have a moderator that has***!

Here is a brief checklist before the conversation:

1. Run your clearing as soon as possible.

2. Try not to assume or jump to conclusions before the clearing.

3. Understand where you are in the drama triangle Villain, Victim, Hero [*bit.ly/drama-video*] and brush up on Radical responsibility.

4. Before starting, ask, "am I above or below the line?" [*bit.ly/locate-video*]

5. Use the template—seriously. The formula works.

6. Have the courage to state how you feel and what you need. People are drawn to each other's vulnerability but repelled by their own. Vulnerability isn't weakness.

7. Expect people to extend you the same courtesy. If someone makes you feel bad for stating your needs and feelings, then they don't belong at Clearbit.

Running a clearing conversation

The goal is to reveal yourself, own your projection, and re-establish connection. For effectiveness, stick to the script.

Most of the time there are three parties to the conversation:

1. A person clearing the issue

2. A person listening to understand

3. A moderator managing the conversation (who ideally has either run one before or been trained by someone who has)

You begin by creating resolution.

Time and location
Clearing conversations should be run at a time and a place that are convenient to all parties. It's important that everyone is in a good "head space."

Ideally these conversations are run in person and everyone is physically present. This is because humans naturally trust each other more when they're in the same vicinity. However, this is not always possible, and a remote clearing is better than no clearing.

Create resolution together
All parties look at each other and affirm the following (a nod is fine):

* I commit to curiosity and letting go of being right

* I commit to taking 100% responsibility for the issue

* I commit to creating a win-for-all resolution

Next, the parties commit that the other represents an important and valued relationship.

Script for person clearing the issue
It's important to stick to the following script (and the moderator should ensure this). For introverts (e.g., a lot of engineers) we find clearings more successful when people pre-prepare and write down their answers to the script. Other personality types prefer talking through the script verbally. Use whatever works, but make sure you keep to the script.

1. "The specific **FACTS** are..." (Recordable facts; not judgments)

2. "A **STORY** I make up about [you/me/the group] is..."

3. "My **FEELING** is..." (Angry, Sad, Scared, Creative, Joyful)

4. "I specifically **WANT**..." (This is not a demand or entitlement but instead a way to be known)

5. "How I **CREATED** this disconnection with you is..."

6. **PROJECTION:** "The part of me I see in you that I have an aversion/attraction to is..."

Script for person listening to understand
"What I hear you saying is..." (Reflect or paraphrase without interpretation) "Is that **RIGHT**?" (If not, reflect again) "Is there **MORE**?" (Ask with curiosity)

"Are you **CLEAR**? Have you said everything you have to say and felt everything you have to feel?" (If yes, move on. If not, go back to "Is there more?")

Is there a **NEXT ACTION** step? (If yes, who will do what by when?)

Appreciate the person for choosing to clear the issue.

If the listener has an issue, it is recommended that you take some time to pause and then switch roles.

Post clearing

If the clearing has been run well, then both sides will have felt heard by the other. This is the first step in rebuilding trust.

You may have a bunch of action items coming out of the clearing that one or both parties have committed to do. It's important that these are written down during the meeting and ratified by all parties (otherwise there may be disagreements about what was agreed upon).

The story in my head

Stories are powerful. They're at the underpinnings of our entire society, from concepts like money to countries to laws to trade agreements. Mutually agreed-upon, shared stories allow humans, separated by thousands of miles, to collaborate.

Collaboration is the secret to our species' success. Collaboration is how we turned rocks into iPhones. Collaboration took us from the first human flight to landing on the moon within 60 years. Collaboration laid the building blocks of modern society. Stories mix the mortar keeping it all together.

How stories evolved

Why did we evolve to be this way? The latest scientific research suggests we evolved the narrator part of our brain in order to predict what other people are going to do next. As you might imagine, being able to predict someone's next move and plan a few steps ahead of them is a distinct evolutionary advantage.

The tricky part is, we have no way of absolutely knowing the future. So instead our mind creates predictions. Every waking moment, our mind is making predictions about the future and then turning those predictions into stories.

For example, let's say you see a car driving erratically. Immediately your mind offers up a few stories. Perhaps the driver is drunk, incapacitated, or old? Perhaps they're texting? Or perhaps they're a nurse just off night shift? Without further evidence, we have no way of knowing, but our mind offers up a buffet of options in the meantime.

It is precisely because stories are so powerful that we should be wary of them. We are so sure that our stories are true, even though the source of these stories, our brain's predictor machine, is inherently error prone. And, if we are not careful, these stories can turn into facts in our minds.

The story in my head

Hang around Clearbit's office long enough and you are bound to hear the phrase "the story in my head is ...". What is the reason for that? There are two concepts behind this:

1. Our assumptions about the world are often flawed.

2. It is better to talk in absolute truths.

Hopefully at this point we have convinced you of the first concept, that the stories in your head are just stories and therefore prone to all the biases and shortcuts baked into the human condition.

Why is it better to talk in absolute truths? To do otherwise would be to hold up your assumptions as truer than the assumptions of others. This is a roadblock to communication and collaboration because you will get hung up arguing. We need to make a clear distinction between facts we know to be true and stories that could (or could not) be true.

Hold your stories loosely

When we say "the story in my head is ..." we are being explicit about two things: that whatever we're talking about *is* a story, and that the story is not necessarily true.

It is vitally important that we actually mean those two things. If you are sure that you are right about the "story," then it's no longer a story in your head, it's a "fact" in your head. And when you start believing your stories are your truth, then you shut out all creativity.

Talk about your internal truths

There are only two types of inarguable truths: facts and internal truths. Facts are things that, through a process of first principles, have been proven beyond reasonable doubt to be true. Internal truths are what you think and feel.

When you are talking about things that aren't clearly facts, it is better to talk about what you observed, what you felt, and the story in your head versus stating a potentially disputable assumption as if it were fact.

🌱 Performance improvement plans (PIPS)

Performance improvement plans (PIPs) are given to low performers with a view to improving their performance rather than being fired.

It is extremely important to manage PIPs effectively. We don't use PIPs for show. This is a genuine opportunity for the employee to improve, and the ideal outcome is for the employee to go on to do great work at Clearbit. Indeed, this is the case for many of the people we put on PIPs at Clearbit.

We want to show the people who work here that nobody is let go on a whim, and that we have a genuine desire to work together and help people improve. Firing someone without a PIP is reserved for situations where either misconduct has occurred or we truly believe that the employee is not likely to complete a PIP.

When do people get put on a PIP?

Someone will be placed on a PIP when they have shown a pattern of not showing any improvement after receiving a lot of critical feedback. We only put people on PIPs when we believe they have the potential to improve.

Nobody should be surprised when they are put on a PIP. They will have received multiple rounds of documented feedback regarding a specific issue that has been labeled as PIP-level critical by their manager during their one-on-ones.

Some examples of this could be many pull requests not being merged because of bad quality/direction, badly missing sales quotas, or a pattern of negligence or not caring about your work.

This type of feedback is different from the weekly "I like that/I wish that" feedback that we share for personal and professional development. PIP-level feedback must be clearly labeled in Asana or email. The key here is to preserve and document your critical feedback in a non-arguable way. Remember, the PIP is a plan for improvement and not where you are documenting your critical feedback.

What are the details of a PIP?

PIPs are confidential and will only be discussed with you, your manager, and the leadership team.

A PIP will last at least two weeks, and could last up to a month. PIPs are written plans with clear, achievable milestones and realistic due dates. Each week, the PIP'ed employee will meet with their manager, who will let them know in writing how they are performing against those milestones. Our aim is to give people the tools and help they need to complete the PIP successfully.

I'm considering a PIP for my report now. What do I do?

Talk to your manager and HR to discuss the issue, clarify what you have done so far, and discuss what the next steps should be. If it is determined that a PIP is the appropriate next step, you will be asked to fill out this PIP Template [*bit.ly/clearbit-pip*] and review it again with your manager and HR before delivering.

 **Firing**

Sadly, there will be times when we have to fire people. This is always unpleasant for everyone, but less bad than having a poor performer bringing the team down (or worse, overburdening your best performer to the point where they leave).

The most important thing to hold in mind is that the decision to fire someone is not a judgement of someone's character (except, of course, in clear cases of negligence or fraud). Nor is it a judgement on their worth as a person. It is only a judgement on their work for the specific role we hired them to do at this specific company.

There are lots of reasons why someone isn't performing. Perhaps you hired them into the wrong role. Or perhaps they didn't gel with the team. Or perhaps their values didn't align with the company's. Or perhaps the company scaled beyond their talents. All of these are perfectly valid reasons to part ways and don't represent a moral failing.

It is quite possible that whoever you are firing is going to go on and do great work for another company. Indeed, it is quite possible that a couple of years down the road, they view being fired as one of the best things that happened to them (although usually this point falls flat at the time).

No surprises

By the time you fire someone, it should be pretty clear to everyone that things aren't working out. For a start, your report will have been on a PIP for at least a few weeks. If you start firing people out of the blue, then everyone else wonders who's next, they get scared, and their performance suffers.

Notify your manager and then Clearbit's People Ops team. They will take you through the process and help you set up a meeting with everyone who needs to attend.

What to say

Our People Ops team will give you a script to run through with your report. Here is an example [*bit.ly/clearbit-fire*] of what this will look like. This will include the benefits we offer, their severance, and next steps. It's important to remember that this meeting is about them, not you. Don't talk about how it's such a hard day for you—we can assure you it's worse for them.

Exit interview

In most cases, we run an exit interview with anyone who leaves the company, whether or not their exit is of their own volition. This is because these interviews can glean important information on steps the company could take to improve.

 "I find exit interviews to be chock-full of insights on what departing employees really think about the company. They are typically eager to share their views. Not all opinions are agreeable. Some are misperceptions. But even misperceptions inform us how poorly we did in communicating context that led to information asymmetry.

The post-exit interview is often a missed opportunity to strengthen trust. I use these opportunities to share desensitized feedback with the org, acknowledging what we heard, and then mount a campaign to address our failures and deliver on our promise."

— *Ye Cheng, VP of Engineering at Paciolan*

Our People Ops team will run this interview and share the results with you.

8. CONSCIOUSNESS

— Above/below the line

At Clearbit, we practice a type of management called Conscious Leadership, a set of principles designed to promote curiosity. The authors behind the movement have written a book, The 15 Commitments of Conscious Leadership [*bit.ly/15-commitments*], which we highly recommend to anyone joining the company.

Conscious Leadership is about being more interested in learning than being right. When our egos make us afraid to be wrong, that fear leads us to defend our ideas at all costs, and to work too hard to convince others that we are right—often with anger.

Conscious Leadership is about recognizing when these emotions (fear, anger, sadness) have gripped our thought processes, releasing these emotions and shifting back to a state of curiosity where we are receptive to all ideas and creativity, even if they seem to contradict our own.

It is in a state of playful curiosity that truly elegant solutions are achieved.

The following is an abbreviated excerpt from the book. This short excerpt will not do it justice, though, so please consider buying the book and supporting the Conscious Leadership Group's [*conscious.is*] work.

Leading from above the line

At any point, a leader is either above the line or below the line. If you are above it, you are leading consciously, and if you are below it, you are not. Above the line, one is open, curious, and committed to learning. Below the line, one is closed, defensive, and committed to being right.

ABOVE THE LINE

OPEN   CURIOUS   COMMITTED TO LEARNING

BELOW THE LINE

CLOSED   DEFENSIVE   COMMITTED TO BEING RIGHT

Many people lead from below the line – it's a common state stemming from millions of years of evolution. As soon as we sense the first whiff of conflict, our lizard brain kicks in. Fear and anger rise up, we get defensive, and we double down on being right. At this point we're firmly below the line.

Knowing that you're below the line is more important than being below the line. The first mark of conscious leadership is self-awareness and the search for truth. The second is pausing, taking a second, and shifting yourself into an open and curious state, and rising above the line.

Shifting

Shifting is moving from closed to open, from defensive to curious, from wanting to be right to wanting to learn, and from fighting for the survival of the individual ego to leading from a place of security and trust.

Shifting first requires a degree of emotional intelligence, realizing that you're feeling below the line (angry/scared), and then taking a moment to pause before reacting.

To shift from below to above the line, we suggest focusing on your breathing and taking a few big breaths in and out. Alternatively, to get the blood moving, take a walk around the room. If you're in a meeting and you sense the group getting below the line, ask them to take a second to pause and stretch—this does wonders for group dynamics.

Conscious Principles

The following are principles to live your life by in order to shift yourself above the line.

Taking radical responsibility

> *I commit to taking full responsibility for the circumstances of my life and for my physical, emotional, mental, and spiritual well-being. I commit to supporting others as they take full responsibility for their lives.*

Taking full responsibility for one's circumstances (physically, emotionally, mentally, and spiritually) is the foundation of true personal and relational transformation. Blame, shame, and guilt all come from toxic fear. Toxic fear drives the victim-villain-hero triangle, which keeps leaders and teams below the line.

Conscious leaders and teams take full responsibility—radical responsibility—instead of placing blame. Radical responsibility means locating the cause and control of our lives in ourselves, not in external events.

Instead of asking who's to blame, conscious leaders ask, "What can we learn and how can we grow from this?" Conscious leaders are open to the possibility that instead of controlling and changing the world, perhaps the world is just right the way it is. This creates huge growth opportunities on a personal and organization level.

Learning through curiosity

I commit to growing in self-awareness. I commit to regarding every interaction as an opportunity to learn. I commit to curiosity as a path to rapid learning.

Self-awareness and learning agility are known to create sustained success in leaders—they form the foundation of conscious leadership.

Conscious leaders are passionately committed to knowing themselves, which is the basis of their willingness to live in a state of curiosity. At any point, leaders are either above the line (open, curious, and committed to learning) or below the line (defensive, closed and committed to being right).

Being "right" doesn't cause drama, but wanting, proving, and fighting to be "right" does. Even though conscious leaders get defensive like everyone else, they regularly interrupt this natural reactivity by pausing to breathe, accept, and shift.

Feeling all feelings

I commit to feeling my feelings all the way through to completion. They come, and I locate them in my body, then I move, breathe, and vocalize them so they release all the way through.

Great leaders learn to access all three centers of intelligence: the head, the heart, and the gut.

Resisting and repressing feelings is standard operating procedure in most organizations. Feelings are viewed as negative and a distraction to good decision making and leadership.

Conscious leaders know that feelings are natural and expressing them is healthy. They know that emotion is energy in motion; feelings are simply physical sensations.

The four primary emotions are anger, fear, sadness, joy. Knowing how to express them all of the way through to completion helps us develop emotional intelligence. Each primary emotion has a unique energy pattern and set of sensations in and on the body. Every feeling we experience invites us in a specific way to grow in awareness and knowing. Repressing, denying, or recycling emotions creates physical, psychological, and relationship problems.

To release emotion, first locate the sensation in the body and then vocalize the feeling.

Conscious leaders learn to locate, name, and release their feelings. They know that feelings not only add richness and color to life but are also an essential ally to successful leadership.

Speaking candidly

*I commit to saying what is true for me. I commit to being a
person to whom others can express themselves with candor.*

Leaders and teams have found that seeing reality clearly is essential to
being successful. In order to see reality clearly, leaders and organizations
need everyone to be truthful and not lie about or withhold information.
They need candor. Candor is the revealing of all thoughts, feelings, and
sensations in an honest, open, and aware way.

Speaking candidly increases the probability that leaders and teams can
collectively see reality more clearly. Withholding is refraining from
revealing everything to all relevant parties. Withholding also decreases
energy in leaders, and this often shows up as boredom or lethargy in
them and relational disconnection in the team.

Rather than withholding, conscious leaders practice revealing. They
reveal not because they are right, but because they wish to be known.
Through this transparency, they create connection and open learning.
Conscious listening is one of the most important skills for effective
leadership: by identifying our listening "filters," we can let go of them and
become fully present to the expression of the other person.

Conscious listening takes courage: we must listen for the content (head
center), the emotions (heart center), and the base desire (gut center)
being expressed by the other person. It is best to start with candor in
relationships only when you have a shared commitment to it, along with
the necessary skills, including being able to speak unarguably.

Eliminating gossip

I commit to ending gossip, talking directly to people with whom I have a concern, and encouraging others to talk directly to people with whom they have an issue or concern.

Even though gossip has long been a part of office culture, it is a key indicator of an unhealthy organization and one of the fastest ways to derail motivation and creativity.

Gossip is a statement about another made by someone with negative intent or a statement the speaker would be unwilling to share in exactly the same way if that person were in the room.

Gossip is an attempt to validate the righteousness of a person's thinking and is below the line; it is not a comment designed to serve the person being discussed.

People gossip to gain validation, control others and outcomes, avoid conflict, get attention, feel included, and make themselves right by making others wrong. In short, people usually gossip out of fear. If you gossip, clean it up by revealing your participation in the gossip to everyone involved.

When leaders and teams learn to speak candidly with each other, they benefit from the direct feedback about issues within the organization that otherwise could derail creative energy and productive collaboration.

Integrity

I commit to the masterful practice of integrity, including acknowledging all authentic feelings, expressing the unarguable truth, keeping my agreements, and taking 100% responsibility.

Integrity is the practice of keeping agreements, taking responsibility, revealing authentic feelings, and expressing unarguable truths. It is essential to thriving leaders and organizations.

Conscious leaders are impeccable with their agreements. They make clear agreements, keep them, renegotiate them when needed, and clean them up when broken. Integrity is fundamental to conscious leadership and successful thriving organizations.

Generating appreciation

> *I commit to living in appreciation, fully opening to both receiving and giving appreciation.*

Committing to appreciation, along with avoiding entitlement, helps leaders and organizations grow value and connection in the workplace.

Appreciation consists of two parts: sensitive awareness and an increase in value.

Entitlement arises when rewards and benefits become an expectation instead of a preference. Living in appreciation has two branches: being open to fully receiving appreciation and being able to fully give appreciation. For most, it is more difficult and people are more afraid to receive appreciation than to give it. To avoid receiving appreciation, people strategically deflect it. Masterful appreciation is sincere, unarguable, specific, and succinct.

Appreciation allows the unique gifts in the community to be recognized.

Living a life of play and rest

I commit to creating a life of play, improvisation, and laughter.
I commit to seeing all of life unfold easefully and effortlessly. I
commit to maximizing my energy by honoring rest, renewal,
and rhythm.

Creating a life of play, improvisation, and laughter allows life to unfold easily and energy to be maximized. Play is an absorbing, apparently purposeless activity that provides enjoyment and suspends self-consciousness and a sense of time.

It is also self-motivating and makes you want to do it again. An imposed nose-to-the-grindstone culture will lead to higher levels of stress, guilt, employee burnout, and turnover. Energy exerted with this type of "hard work" is wrought with effort and struggle, whereas energy exerted through play is energizing.

Most leaders resist play because they think they will fall behind if they aren't seriously working hard. Organizations that take breaks to rest and play are actually more productive and creative. Energy is maximized when rest, renewal, and personal rhythms are honored.

Conscious leaders who value and encourage an atmosphere of play and joy within themselves and in their organizations create high-functioning, high-achieving cultures.

Exploring the opposite

I commit to seeing that the opposite of my story is as true as
or truer than my original story. I recognize that I interpret the
world around me and give my stories meaning.

Conscious leaders practice simple ways to question the beliefs that cause suffering, starting with "Is it true?" and "Can I absolutely know it is true?" The turnaround exercise allows leaders to practice shifting their beliefs from knowing to curiosity. When conscious leaders let go of the righteousness of their beliefs, they are then open to curiosity and align with their deepest desires.

😾 Avoiding politics & gossip

We've never met anyone who says "I love corporate politics." So why is it so prevalent in some companies? The answer is, it all comes down to incentives.

Let's define what we mean by politics: *people advancing their careers or agendas by means other than merit and contribution.* There are lots of different kinds of politics but this form seems the most bothersome.

It all starts from the top. A CEO creates politics by encouraging and sometimes incentivizing political behavior—often unintentionally. Once everyone sees that political behavior is not only accepted, but encouraged, it starts spreading throughout your company like a cancer.

Let's take a few examples to try and demonstrate how you might unintentionally create politics.

Scenario #1

A senior employee comes to you with a competitive offer in hand, asking for a promotion. You investigate the situation and decide that, since you really don't want to lose this employee, you will cave and give them a promotion.

You have just created a strong incentive for political behavior.

After you fold, three things happen:

1. Word gets out that "all you need to do to get a raise is to ask for it." You have sent out the message that raises aren't tied to performance.

2. Less aggressive employees will be denied a raise simply by being apolitical.

3. The lesson to your team is that the most politically astute employees get raises. Prepare for more politics!

If folding to raise requests creates an incentive for politics, what's the alternative?

1. Put a process around raises. Do them annually, and don't make them out of band.

2. Create a leveling system that can be referred to objectively.

3. Never cave to people who have competing offers.

Scenario #2

Your team is growing, and to minimize your number of direct reports, you decide to promote one of your ICs. You announce your decision to your team, expecting them to be relieved that they're going to see more managerial attention.

You have just created a strong incentive for political behavior.

Whenever you promote someone, your team will evaluate whether merit or political favors (e.g. favoritism) yielded it. If it's not clearly the former, the latter is assumed.

They generally react in these three ways:

1. They sulk and feel undervalued.

2. They outwardly disagree, campaign against that person, and undermine them in their new position.

3. They attempt to copy any political behavior they perceive as generating the promotion.

So what's the correct solution here?

1. Explain the problem to your team: you're swamped.

2. Create a job spec for the managerial position, and list objective criteria for anyone applying to be evaluated by.

3. Run a full interview process, considering internal and external candidates.

4. Now you have demonstrated that the promotion was due to merit.

> "A peer-written nomination in the form of a promo packet can also demonstrate merit. It achieves the same result as the interview process (which would've been conducted by a panel consisting of peers), minus the pressure of interviewing well. It also has the added benefit of surfacing candidates who shun self-promotion, but has quietly built up a large sphere of influence without authority."
>
> — *Ye Cheng, VPE Paciolan*

Gossip

Like politics, it requires constant vigilance to prevent gossip spreading through your company. Unlike with politics, some people actually enjoy gossiping. For a start, don't hire those people. Even still, there are active measures you can deploy to prevent gossip.

Let's be precise again and define what we mean by gossip: *saying negative comments behind someone's back without an intention of helping them.*

The answer to gossip is simply to have a zero-tolerance policy.

If you hear gossip about a person:

* Offer to pull the gossiped party directly into the room so the message can be repeated in front of them.

* Or ask for an assurance that they resolve this matter directly with the responsible individual.

If you find yourself gossiping about a person:

* Resolve to address the issue as soon as possible directly with the relevant person.

* Set a dedicated meeting or make a note to bring it up in a one-on-one.

* Potentially ask for a clearing session with a mediator.

 Company values

How do two people who've never met each other collaborate? This is quite an interesting question because it strikes at the heart of why the human race has been so successful compared to our fellow animals: collaboration at scale.

Collaboration allows us to perform feats that would be impossible to perform individually. For example, scaled collaboration allows us to build complicated machines, like tractors, that semi-automate farming and manage complex supply chains so we don't spend the majority of our day gathering food.

So what goes into collaboration at scale? It clearly involves a degree of good communication. And good communication relies on speed and bandwidth. As the speed of communication has steadily increased through the ages (from sending horses → letters → wires → telephone calls → emails), so has our collaboration improved.

Communication isn't enough though. The USA and Russia had a red hotline to each other throughout the Cold War, but didn't collaborate on much. There's a second ingredient: trust.

Collaboration through trust

If two people have never met each other, how can they trust each other? The answer is, they proxy their trust through a third party. This might be a company or some kind of institution. It doesn't have to physically exist. As long as both parties believe and trust in it, they can outsource their trust for each other and collaborate.

The simplest shared basis for trust between people is money. We invented money because it abstracts away the inconvenience of bartering. As long as both parties have trust in a particular currency, they can use that to collaborate.

For example, the North Koreans and the US couldn't disagree more, politically. But they both trust in the United States dollar, and so they can collaborate on things like hostage negotiations.

This works very effectively for simple collaboration. For more complex financial collaboration, we combine money with legal contracts to proxy our trust to the courts. However, it does lead to a mercenary kind of relationship which, while effective, can lead to individualistic short-term thinking.

Consider a salesman motivated purely by commission. They have a part-collaborative, part-contentious relationship with the company they work for. While they rely on the company to create a valuable product they can sell, their focus is on their quarterly commission. They are competing with their colleagues and they are not incentivized to care about the long-term prospects of the company. Indeed, if the company goes through a rough patch, their incentive is to jump ship and find something easier to sell.

There are ways to solve parts of this. For example, issuing stock options to your team ties their performance to the long-term prospects of the company, which in turn incentives longer-term thinking and behavior. But you can still run into the mercenary aspect of a purely financial relationship: reduced loyalty.

So to get scaled collaboration, we need to combine financial incentives with something less transactional. There are a variety of tried and tested ways of doing this, but they boil down to three things: shared mission, shared values, and a close-knit community.

Mission vs. values

We all crave purpose and connection in life. Working on a mission you believe in with a group of people who share your values is a combination that is more intoxicating than any financial reward.

If a mission is what we do, then values are how we go about doing it. Our mission is our north star, and our values help us assemble a team, plan, prioritize, collaborate, and build the spaceship to get there.

While people may share our mission, if they don't share our values, it'll be impossible to work together. That's why it's very important to screen for values during the interview process.

They actually make hiring easier because they're a great filter, not just on our end but also on the candidates' end. We present candidates with our values and if they don't align with them, they tend to opt out. And that's ultimately a win-win all around.

We also use our values when deliberating. Often we have to make decisions that juggle competing company priorities. Our company values often show us the way.

We like to celebrate our company values every week by highlighting a *person of the week* who has demonstrated a particular company value. This helps us talk about our values at every all-hands.

Our values

1. **Care (Give a shit).** Empathize with our customers (and each other). Take the time to understand our customers' and colleagues' frustrations, needs, and desires.

2. **Craft (Master it).** Own your craft. Never stop learning and improving.

3. **Team (Work together).** Teamwork makes the dream work. Fill gaps. There's no such thing as "It's not my job."

4. **Truth (Say it).** Be upfront and candid. Say it like it is. Hold yourself and others accountable.

5. **Initiative (Be resourceful).** Don't wait for permission. Figure it out—or figure out who can.

6. **Fun (Have it).** Don't take yourself too seriously—life is short.

Picking your values

Values come from the team, not the CEO. Matt Mochary puts it well in
The Great CEO Within:

 One misconception CEOs sometimes have is thinking they get
to choose the values. By the time you have thirty or so employees, your company has a set of values whether you like it or
not. It's now your job to codify what's already there. While it is
possible to change a value, it will take a lot of work. Agreeing
on what your values are is the kind of statement that needs
maximum buy-in, so it should involve your whole company.
Send out a survey and gather contributions from everyone.
Ask your team to suggest both a value and the name of an
employee who exemplifies it. Then arrange all the suggestions
into common themes, and have your leadership team vote on
the final cut.

Once you have agreed on your values, use them to guide your
hiring and firing. Bring in people who want to live by these
principles, and let go of people who don't. Otherwise, your
values will have no meaning. Distribute your values, print
them out, and repeat them until your team knows them back
to front. Every week at the all-hands meeting, highlight a
value and a person whose actions best exemplify that value
that week.

Further reading

We recommend a talk by Sebastian Deterding on What your designs
say about you. Sebastian delves into the implicit values we push when
creating products.

🧑 Personal values

It's not just companies that have values. People have them too (whether we realize it or not).

Our values are what we use when evaluating big decisions, and they determine how we sit with the consequences of those decisions. Should I go back to grad school? Should I move cities? Should I propose to my partner?

However, what we often don't do is do this intentionally. We internalize values at a subconscious level and they surface as gut feelings. For the most part, we don't use them with intent.

By really understanding your values, you can turn these gut feelings into an intentional framework you can use for evaluating decisions and behaviors. Your values can be your north star, your guiding principles, and the bedrock of how you live your life.

Understanding your values

Rather than intentionally going out and *choosing* your values, you already have a set of values derived from the melting pot of your life experiences, upbringing, mentors, and a whole lot of other sources. You simply have to dig into whatever's there.

Figuring out which values most resonate with you is a fascinating process, since often you will discover interesting contradictions and hierarchies between your chosen values.

 "My two values are growth and freedom. I define growth in terms of a journey of self discovery, and freedom as the ability to forge my destiny on my own terms. I've found that values I thought were fundamental to me, like happiness, are actually derivations of my two core values. I can't be happy unless I am also free and growing. What's interesting is that these two values are often at odds with each other. A large amount of freedom can result in little growth, and vice versa. Plotting a path between the contradictions of the two is part of what makes life interesting."

– *Alex MacCaw*

Take a look at the list of values below from the book Dare to Lead [*bit. ly/daretoleadbrene*] (and by all means, add to these). Now whittle down this list and pick *two values* that resonate the most with you. You may find that there's a hierarchy and that one value is derived from another. In these cases, pick the higher-ranking value.

Why only two? Well, if you have more than a few priorities, you have no priorities. At some point, if everything on the list is important, then nothing is truly a driver for you. It's just a shallow list of feel-good words.

The other thing to realize is that there's no difference between personal and professional values. When it comes to something as fundamental as our values, one can't live a bipolar life.

list of values

Accountability
Achievement
Adaptability
Adventure
Altruism
Ambition
Authenticity
Balance
Beauty
Being the best
Belonging
Career
Caring
Collaboration
Commitment
Community
Compassion
Competence
Confidence
Connection
Contentment
Contribution
Cooperation
Courage
Creativity
Curiosity
Dignity
Diversity
Environment
Efficiency
Equality
Ethics
Excellence
Fairness
Faith
Family
Financial stability

Forgiveness
Freedom
Friendship
Fun
Future generations
Generosity
Giving back
Grace
Gratitude
Growth
Harmony
Health
Home
Honesty
Hope
Humility
Humor
Inclusion
Independence
Initiative
Integrity
Intuition
Job security
Joy
Justice
Kindness
Knowledge
Leadership
Learning
Legacy
Leisure
Love
Loyalty
Making a difference
Nature
Openness
Optimism
Order
Parenting
Patience
Patriotism
Peace
Perseverance

Personal fulfillment
Power
Pride
Recognition
Reliability
Resourcefulness
Respect
Responsibility
Risk taking
Safety
Security
Self-discipline
Self-expression
Self-respect
Serenity
Service
Simplicity
Spirituality
Sportsmanship
Stewardship
Success
Teamwork
Thrift
Time
Tradition
Travel
Trust
Truth
Understanding
Uniqueness
Usefulness
Vision
Vulnerability
Wealth
Well-being
Wholeheartedness
Wisdom

Write your own:

_____

_____

Whittling down a list of values can work well, but it's not the right technique for everyone. Eric Feldman suggests a different approach [*bit. ly/values-feldman*] based on analyzing major life experiences.

Living into your values

Now you've picked your values, it's time to think about behaviors that are *in* and *out* of integrity with these values.

Write down three behaviors that support each value, and three slippery behaviors that are outside this value. To get you started, we've listed an example below:

Three behaviors that support Freedom:

- Forging my own path and being curious – see the systems, learn from them, choose pieces that work for me, and walk away from the rest.

- Putting together life plans and goals. Putting up boundaries.

- Being vulnerable. Having confidence in my weird and kinky self.

Three slippery behaviors that are outside Freedom:

- Going with the conventional route just because it's "blessed."

- Using substances/alcohol excessively just to be comfortable in social situations.

- Placing value in social pecking orders and hierarchy.

Lastly, write down three examples of situations where you were fully living each value and three situations when you weren't. These might be painful to think about, but understanding how your values apply to real-world scenarios will help you live by them.

Living into our values means that we do more than profess our values, we practice them. A value-led life is a life driven with purpose and integrity. Once you have this incredible toolbox, you will be well equipped to deal with decisions, knowing that you will make choices consistent with what's ultimately important to you.

 We are all creators

One of the most profound realizations you can come to in life is the idea that you are a creator. Truly understanding and living this will have a massively positive impact on your life, from your relationships to your career to your happiness.

There are two main ways of looking at the world: things happen either *to me* or *by me.*

To me

If I am in the *to me* state, I see myself "at the effect of," meaning that the cause of my condition is outside me. It is happening *to me.* Whether I see the cause as another person, circumstance, or condition, I believe I'm being acted upon by external forces.

People in *to me* are at the mercy of the markets, competitors, team members who "don't get it," suppliers, the weather, their own mood, their spouse, their children, their bank account, and their health, to name a few.

They believe that these external realities are responsible for their unhappiness (if only my spouse weren't mean, I'd be happy); for their failures (if only my sales team would work harder, our top line would go up); and for their insecurities (if only I had more validation from my boss, I would feel more secure at my job).

People in a *to me* mindset do not take responsibility for themselves and instead blame others, or external factors. This is because it's far less effort to play the victim than to take responsibility.

People consistently stuck in a *to me* mindset are often playing into a wider archetype they have about themselves, such as "I failed because I'm a failure." Ultimately, beneath this lies an urge to elicit sympathy from others, and again requires less effort than taking responsibility.

By me

When people shift from below the line to above it, they move from the *to me* to the *by me* state—from living in victim consciousness to living in creator consciousness and from being at the mercy of to "consciously creating with." Instead of believing that the cause of their experience is outside themselves, they believe that they are the cause of their experience.

People in a *by me* state choose to see that everything in the world is unfolding perfectly for their learning and development. Nothing has to be different. They see that what is happening is for them.

Instead of asking "Why is this happening to me?" the *by me* leader asks questions like, "What can I learn from this?" "How is this situation 'for me'?" "How am I creating this and keeping this going?"

Shifting

To shift out of a *to me* mindset, we first need to realize we're in one—and take a deep breath. Then we need to choose to take radical responsibility for whatever is happening in our lives, to let go of blaming anyone, and to approach problems with curiosity.

Of course, this is easier said than done, and it's unlikely that just reading this chapter is going to magically change your attitude in life. This is part of a deeper exploration, so we recommend reading the books The Courage to Be Disliked [*bit.ly/disliked-courage*] and the 15 Commitments of Conscious Leadership [*bit.ly/15-commitments*] to start that journey.

Long-term shifting

The most successful people in life manage to approach most of their problems with a *by me* mindset. They realize that they are creative forces in their lives and that they can have a massive impact on how their lives play out.

The only way we've seen to fundamentally shift to a long-term creator mindset is via goal setting. Set small goals, achieve them, and then set larger ones. Prove to yourself that you can achieve things you set your mind to. This builds up the personal confidence needed to feel comfortable in the *by me* mindset.

THE HIGHLIGHTS

Do

1. Attract, nurture, coach, and retain talent.

2. Communicate the next most important challenge the company/team is facing.

3. Set goals, not tasks.

4. Be the tiebreaker when your team can't reach consensus.

5. Be the information hub. Know what everyone is working on, and connect the dots that wouldn't otherwise get connected.

6. Create a feedback-safe environment where people feel heard, and celebrate critical feedback. Lead by example.

7. Keep an eye on your team's health and happiness.

8. Hire the right people to succeed at the team goals and ensure that the strengths of everyone on the team match their roles.

9. Give your team a clear path to progress in their careers.

Don't

1. Micromanage your teams work or daily output (creative work isn't an assembly line). If you find yourself supervising too often, you've hired the wrong people.

2. Publicly shame (ever).

3. Accept gossip or intra-team politics.

4. Ship your own projects before you enable your team.

5. Spend your time doing too much IC work. For every direct report, dedicate roughly 15% of your time to managing them. A manager with 7 reports should have very little bandwidth for IC work.

Motivation

1. Tech work is a seller's market: people work for you because they believe in you. Access to their talent is a privilege.

2. Authority isn't bestowed freely. It's earned by repeatedly making good decisions.

3. Don't make decisions unless you have to. Whenever possible, allow the team to explore ideas and make decisions on its own.

4. Determine how much buy-in a decision needs. Delegate accordingly.

5. Help make decisions when necessary; few things are as demoralizing as a stalled team.

6. Don't shoot down ideas until it's necessary. Create an environment where everyone feels safe to share and explore ideas.

Hiring

1. A manager's output = The output of her team + The output of the neighboring teams under her influence.

2. You are measured, as a leader, on how many people you need on your team to achieve the desired output (i.e., your managerial leverage). In other words, how much are you able to do with as few people as possible?

3. When adding someone, ask yourself if someone is:

   » Individually so productive that they raise the average productivity of your team?

   » Acting as a multiplier to everyone else on the team?

   If the answer is no to both questions, don't add them to your team.

People

1. Hire great people, then trust them completely. Default to trust, then let anyone go who doesn't live up to that trust.

2. You're the one who makes final hiring and firing decisions. Everything that happens on your team is your responsibility.

3. If you feel something's wrong, you're probably right. Trust your gut.

4. If you find yourself blaming someone, you're probably wrong. Nobody wakes up and tries to do a bad job. 95% of the time you can resolve your feelings by running a respectful clearing session.

5. People make emotional decisions 90%–100% of the time. Including you. All intellectual arguments have strong emotional undercurrents. You'll be dramatically more efficient once you learn to figure out what those are.

6. Most people don't easily share their emotions. It's your job to pull them out and set the example by sharing your own.

7. Have the courage to say what everyone knows to be true but isn't saying.

8. Discover and fix cultural problems your team may not be aware of. Have the courage to say what everyone should know but doesn't.

9. Unless you're a sociopath, firing people is so hard you'll invent excuses not to do it. If you're constantly wondering if someone's a good fit for too long, have the courage to do what you know is right.

Zone of Genius

1. People's performance consists of a mixture of skills, strengths, and talents.

   » A **strength** is anything that gives you energy.

   » A **talent** is an innate ability that can't be taught.

   » A **skill** is a competency that can be taught.

» When all three are aligned, we are in our zone of genius.

2. It's often clear when talent isn't present. Strengths are less clear. Beware the zone of competence, where someone is good at doing a function but doesn't get energy from it—it will ultimately lead to burn out.

   » Every person is unique.

   » You can't turn weaknesses into strengths, or create talent where there is none. These things are innate.

   » All you can teach are skills. Direct your feedback there.

   » Focus on doubling down on someone's existing Zone of Genius.

   » Align people's work with what they're already good at.

   » There is no such thing as an A player in isolation. There is an A team, where each member on the team brings distinct value.

3. Ask yourself whether this person is capable of doing the work you want them to do if their life depended on it. Is it a question of motivation or a question of capability?

   » If their life depended on it and they could do it, then that's on you as a leader not providing the proper motivation.

   » If however, they would be unable to do it even if their life depended on it, then that is your mistake as a manager for expecting them to be able to.

Decisions

1. Don't judge too quickly; you're right less often than you think. Even if you're sure you're right in any given case, wait until everyone's opinion is heard. Remember that you are the loudest voice in the room.

2. Once everyone is heard, summarize all points of view so clearly that people say "Thanks, I wish I'd thought of putting it that way." List any points of agreement with each view, and state what you've learned from everyone. Then make your decision.

3. Set the expectation that once a decision has been made, everyone gets on board [*bit.ly/disagree-commit*].

4. Reopen the discussion if there is significant new information.

5. Don't let people pressure you into decisions you don't believe in. They'll hold *you* responsible for them later, and they'll be right. Decisions are your responsibility.

6. Believe in yourself. You can't lead a cavalry charge if you think you look funny on a horse.

Conflict

1. When disagreement gets personal or people don't accept well-reasoned decisions, it turns into conflict.

2. Most conflict happens because people don't feel heard or don't feel like they have agency to control their world.

3. Sit down with each person and ask them how they feel. Listen carefully. Then ask again. And again. Then summarize what they said back to them. Most of the time that will solve the problem.

4. If the conflict persists after you've gone to reasonable lengths to hear everyone out and fix problems, it's time for a clearing conversation.

Clearing conversations

1. Run your clearing as soon as possible.

2. Try not to assume or jump to conclusions before the clearing.

3. Understand where you are in the drama triangle: Villain, Victim, Hero [*bit.ly/drama-video*]

4. Before starting, ask, "am I above or below the line?" [*bit.ly/locate-video*]

5. Use the template — seriously. The formula works.

6. Have the courage to state how you feel and what you need. People are drawn to one another's vulnerability but repelled by their own. Vulnerability isn't weakness.

7. Expect people to extend you the same courtesy. If someone makes you feel bad for stating your needs and feelings, then they don't belong at Clearbit.

Setting boundaries

1. People will push and prod to discover your boundaries. Knowing when to stand back and when to stand firm is half the battle.

2. Occasionally someone will push too far. When they do, you have to show a rough edge or you'll lose authority with your team.

3. A firm "That's not ok here" or "I'm not OK with that" is usually enough.

4. Don't laugh things off if you don't feel like laughing them off. Have the courage to show your true emotions.

5. If you have to firmly say "I'm not ok with that" too many times to the same person, it's your job to fire them.

APPENDIX

Recommended reading

The problems encountered in starting, growing and running a company have been encountered by thousands of people before.

Fortunately dozens of successful CEOs and business leaders have written down their lessons learned in book form. These books teach us almost every important aspect of running a business and managing people.

While there are hundreds of such books, the following are our favorites. Note that by some of the books, we have indicated they are *required reading* by all managers at Clearbit.

Title	Authors	Tags	Description	Reading hours	Synopsis
The 15 Commitments of Conscious Leadership	Diana Chapman	Culture, Required Reading	Companies can become good using the hard skills outlined in the books above. To become great, a company must become curious and open to learning. This book shows how to do that.	10	*bit.ly/ synopsis-15*
Nonviolent Communication: A Language of Life	Marshall Rosenberg	Culture, Required Reading	Gives you a framework for communicating feedback effectively.	10	

Title	Authors	Tags	Description	Reading hours	Synopsis
Who: The A Method for Hiring	Geoff Smart	Recruiting, Required Reading	Excellent recruiting process that maximizes the likelihood of hiring A players only, and then ensuring their success at the company.	6	
Principles: Life and Work	Ray Dalio	Culture, Individual Productivity	How to live a more objective and principled life. Seeking the truth and being curious about possibilities.	10	*bit.ly/synopsis-principles*
Getting Things Done	David Allen	Individual Productivity	Personal productivity; describes using pen/paper, simply translate that to Evernote or another electronic tool. Using this system will make you sleep better. It takes several days to fully implement the system, but is very much worth that investment.	10	*hamberg. no/gtd*
One Minute Manager	Ken Blanchard	Organizational Productivity	Simple reporting structure that works. Simple enough that you can have all your team members read it. I recommend that you do. (Some of it is obviously dated. Ignore those parts.)	0.5	*bit.ly/ synopsis-one*
High Output Management	Andy Grove	Organizational Productivity	The classic tech management book. A lot more detail than 1-Minute Manager, but essentially the same structure.	10	*bit.ly/synopsis-output*

Title	Authors	Tags	Description	Reading hours	Synopsis
The Hard Things about Hard Things	Ben Horowitz	Organizational Productivity	Says how great High Output Management is, and then talks about what to do in some very specific and ugly situations that no other books discuss.	6	*bit.ly/ synopsis-hard*
Disciplined Entrepreneurship	Bill Aulet	Sales & Marketing	Painful, but very necessary step-by-step guide to determining who your real customer is, what solution they want, and how to market and sell to them. If you only read and apply one of these books, make it this one.	12	*bit.ly/synopsis-disciplined*
Never Split the Difference	Chris Voss	Sales & Marketing	Ostensibly about negotiation, but really about how to create deep connection and trust quickly, which is the key to an excellent relationship with your three key constituents: customers (sales), employees (management) and investors (fundraising). This is the best book on sales that I have found.	6	*bit.ly/ synopsis-split*

Title	Authors	Tags	Description	Reading hours	Synopsis
The Courage to Be Disliked	Ichiro Kishimi and Fumitake Koga	Culture, Individual Productivity	Explains Adler's philosophy, a way of taking back control of your emotions and changing your outlook on life.	10	
The Great CEO Within	Matt Mochary and Alex MacCaw	Individual Productivity, Organizational Productivity			

🙍 What does it mean to be an executive?

💡 Leadership is a different skill than management. Leadership is about being proactive, while management is more reactive. As an executive, your role will involve a lot more leadership. The best article we've seen on executive excellence is one by renowned venture capitalist Keith Rabois. It's written by his chief of staff, Delian Asparouhov. Rather than paraphrase it, we're reproducing it in its entirety below.

Part 1: Running yourself

Lead, don't manage

You need to think of yourself as a producer and a leader driving value, not as a manager. Calling yourself a manager implies some level of reactivity. You manage unexpected situations. You lead to ideal outcomes. You want to be active versus reactive. Driving the vehicle versus a passenger observing. You are judged as a leader by your ability to drive output. Yes, unexpected situations will come up, but that should not be your primary modus operandi.

Understand your output

Ok so what does output mean? From Andy Grove (though unfortunately he uses "manager"):

$$\text{A manager's output} = \frac{\text{The output of his organization}}{+} \\ \text{The output of the neighboring organizations under his influence}$$

For example, as the head of product, you are primarily responsible for the pace of product releases and updates. You also have a heavy influence on the output of customer support, most of the customers that write in, do so because of a flaw in the product. Your total output as a leader is both product releases and decreasing the number of tickets due to product flaws.

You are also judged as a leader on how many people you need on your team to achieve your output, i.e. your managerial leverage. How much are you able to do with as few people as possible?

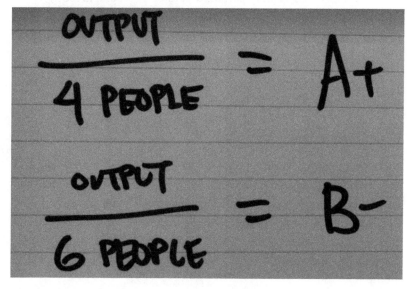

$$\frac{OUTPUT}{4\ PEOPLE} = A+$$

$$\frac{OUTPUT}{6\ PEOPLE} = B-$$

This has implications for how you should think about hiring people to your team. People should either individually be so productive that they raise the average productivity of your team, or act as a multiplier to everyone currently on your team. In either case, make sure your overall productivity increase covers the cost of bringing them on. This prevents leaders from arbitrarily hiring into their team for sake of building up a fiefdom. Want to add someone? Sure, go ahead but remember that it raises the bar on expected total per person output.

Focus on inputs

As a leader you do not want to focus on just your outputs, rather you want to see yourself as a function of your inputs to achieve the optimal output. Jeff Bezos spoke at our CEO summit last year and articulated why this was so important to him at Amazon. If you managed people according to their outputs, then your best people will tackle the short-term conservative projects they know will drive outputs to at least some degree. Instead if you manage to their inputs and clarity of thinking, your best people will focus on projects that have the highest potential upside that is explainable, even if they are risky and totally flop. This is part of why Keith hates OKRs; setting your goal to just 3x your revenue over the year will never lead to your best people doing experiments that might lead to 10x revenue increases. Later on I'll discuss how you can use the clarity of written reports to judge someone's inputs.

Spend time on high leverage activities

In order to maximize your team's output, you need to spend time on the activities that will influence that output the most. For example, at Square, Keith would spend at least 5 hours every week preparing for his pre-sentations at the all-hands meeting on Fridays. That might seem like an inordinate time to spend on a weekly presentation, however if he was able to communicate a single idea that affected how everyone at the company made decisions, then it was absolutely worth it.

This is the first category of high leverage activities, when you have many people affected by one thing, spending a lot of time to perfect it is high leverage. Another example in this category is creating your team's dashboards. Obsessing over the exact layout, font choice, graph types, and colors might seem extreme. However, if it is the dashboard your team looks at every morning when they start work, and what they base their decisions off of, it is critical that it is perfect.

Another category of high leverage activities are when you can have a significant impact on a single person. For example, in his first few months at PayPal, Reid Hoffman sat Keith down and told him that Peter Thiel didn't think Keith was quantitative enough when making arguments. For the next six months, Keith made sure to include metrics in all of his arguments and still thinks about that feedback 16 years later. Being both precise and incredibly candid in your feedback to a single individual can have a massive, and long-term effect and is a very high leverage use of your time.

Optimize your most valuable resource, your time

In order to make sure you are doing high leverage activities, you need to literally review exactly how you are spending your time. Even Ben Franklin, before the days of widespread usage of professional calendars, knew that his most precious resource was his time and needed to allocate it proactively.

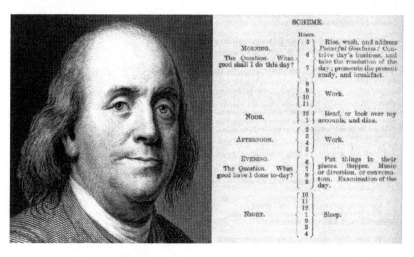

Keith has noticed that two people with similar education, professional history, and skills can have massive long term differences in success based on how well they utilize their scarcest resource, time.

The calendar interfaces we use today actually exacerbate the problem of not optimizing your time. Most executives are entirely reactive to requests for their time and typically let anyone in the organization put meetings wherever they want on the calendar.

You should instead view your calendar as something you proactively manage and design. Each Sunday afternoon, write down your top 3 priorities for the week and design your calendar to spend 80%+ of your time on those priorities. You can leave some "leftover" time on your calendar to fill with the reactive requests.

For example, almost every CEO that we meet with lists recruiting as one of their top 3 priorities. But if we pull up their calendar, most of them have two 45-min coffees and a single 1:1 with their head of talent. If you're only spending 2 hours on recruiting, is it really in your top 3 priorities? Managing your time proactively is very counterintuitive and not how most people operate. You need to constantly check back in every week to not let yourself slip into a reactive mode and perform calendar audits on a regular cadence. That means sitting down and going through your calendar for the past month and categorizing each event into your various priorities, as well as identifying how much of your time was spent on high leverage activities.

Here's a real example from back in the days of Square, when a customer success manager did calendar audits on his team for the upcoming week and edited their calendars. Both times, the team saw an immediate jump in their metrics!

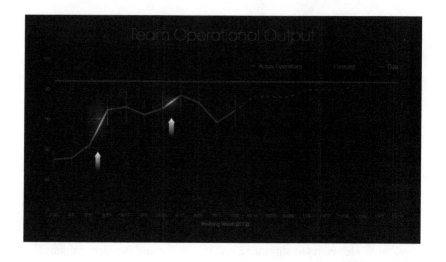

There are a few tactics from production manufacturing that you can also
use to optimize your time. In any manufacturing line, each step of the
process has a different total potential throughput, however the throughput of the entire line is always determined by whichever step has the least
throughput, i.e. the limiting step. In order to improve the throughput
of the entire line, you have to focus all your efforts on improving your
limited step. Any effort dedicated to other steps on the line might help
you down the line, but aren't at all important to work on. Identify the
limiting step in your top priority and make sure that 20-80% of your time
is dedicated to working on it.

Another tactic from manufacturing you can use is to batch together
similar tasks, for example doing all of your 1:1s back to back on the
same day. Mostly because context switching is incredibly costly for most
people. Paul Graham actually discusses this best in Maker's Schedule,
Manager's Schedule [*paulgraham.com/makersschedule.html*]. One thing
to keep in mind, is that to be a great executive, you need to reserve time
for making and thinking. You have to reserve long, uninterrupted time
on your calendar to both think deeply about your strategy, but also for
when you are preparing things that affect many people, i.e. an all-hands
presentation. For example, Mathilde Collin from Front said she blocks off
5 hours every Thursday afternoon [*bit.ly/collin-joy*].

You also want everyone on your team to be proactive about their time management as well. One of the best ways to do this is to present a real-world example of someone on your team who does this well. Walk everyone through an example week on their calendar and point out exactly how they are spending their time. Then have everyone pull out their own calendar and have them go through the same process on their own calendar. Are they batching tasks? Which of the events are high leverage activities? Are there more efficient patterns to create? You should go through this process with your entire team at least once a quarter.

Part 2: Running your team

Gathering information

A critical part of being an effective executive is making the right decision at tough times. Peter Thiel has said that a CEO is largely judged by making the right call about 4 times a year. Doing so without having all the information you need is intellectually bankrupt. Most of your time should be spent gathering information. A lot of that will be fed to you from your direct reports, however any information reaching you is by default going through several layers of filtering. That filtering is not always properly done, so you need to spend time just wandering through your office, picking up on the hallway discussions. You should also meet with skip-levels, i.e. people that report to your direct reports, and get information directly from them. Your goal here is to occasionally tap into the raw information feed of your company, as a sanity-check to make sure no one is filtering something away that is actually very important.

One great way to consistently receive information is to have your team create weekly written reports. Bezos is famous for utilizing this at Amazon with his six page memos [*bit.ly/amazon-memos*]. By writing long-form, you are forced to clarify your exact thinking, and it always exposes any logical fallacies you have. Most of the benefit actually accrues to the writer who is forced to clarify their thoughts, as opposed to the reader. For example, when any of our founders and executives are preparing their board decks for a meeting, they almost always end up discovering something about their business in the process of digging into their metrics.

Simplify the metrics and objectives

Your goal is to simplify the information you gathered down to only a few key important indicators. These indicators should act as early predictors to your team's eventual output. Ideally early enough that you have time to adjust course when they start to veer off, and fix the problem before it affects your output. You almost always want a pairing indicator to prevent your team from overly optimizing to a single goal. For example if you tell your engineering team that they need to ship an update every two weeks, then you need a pairing indicator that measures the number of features they are actually shipping. Otherwise they will definitely ship every two weeks, but the updates to the product will not be meaningful. A classic example of paired indicators Keith used at Square were fraud loss rate vs false-positive rate. It's very easy to make sure that you don't lose any money to fraud if you treat everyone like a fraudster and subject them to tons of hoops and hurdles to send any money. However this is not a good user experience, as any recent user of PayPal can tell you. PayPal would be well served by optimizing a pairing indicator that measures how often they accuse an innocent person of being a suspect.

Beyond just the indicators, you also need to simplify your team's objective down to a singular goal. If your team tries to focus on everything, they will by default focus on nothing. You also need to have as simple of a logical explanation about why accomplishing this goal will make the biggest difference to the business. High Output Management even has some data which shows that for each step you have to add to this logic, you lose approximately 20-40% of your team's performance.

This is why it is such a high leverage activity to spend countless hours optimizing the dashboards your team looks at every day. If you can make the logical equation in their head as simple and easy to understand as possible, it can lead to massive performance gains in moving the input indicators and, eventually, your team's output.

Simplifying both your indicators and your objectives is incredibly difficult. By default you are ignoring indicators and metrics that are true, and other potential objectives which could also be effective. As part of deciding on which to focus on, you should ask yourself, if I could only move one metric, which would it be and why?

Meetings and Decisions

There are a few different types of meetings, and you should explicitly decide which type of meeting you are having ahead of time. Agendas across all these meetings should be set and sent ahead of time.

The first is 1:1s, which Andy Grove originally pioneered through High Output Management. It might sound basic now, but when he introduced the idea of doing regular 1:1s with your direct reports, it was a very radical idea. 1:1s are done for the sake of the junior person, they should be the ones setting the agenda and should ideally focus on giving guidance on performance. Most importantly the junior person should be flagging potential problems as soon as possible. The earlier you know about a problem, the more degrees of freedom you have to implement a solution. One week before launch, there's not much you can really change.

The second is staff meetings, meaning you meet with all of your most senior leaders. Claire Hughes Johnson has given the defining talk on this topic and I would highly recommend listening to it here [*bit.ly/ meeting-video*]. Your staff meeting should have a predefined agenda that covers a range of topics, each of which should affect at least two people. You should also decide ahead of time how you and your staff will make decisions, for example you can be democratic (majority vote rules), consensus (everyone has to agree), or autocratic (the most senior person makes the call).

The third is decision meetings, which is a subset of what should happen regularly in your staff meetings. When a particularly major decision needs to be made, you can gather your team to discuss what the final call should be. Even if you do democratic or consensus, you should always stick to the "Peers Plus One" model, meaning that there is always one person in the room that is the most senior. This can make sure there is someone responsible for things not getting "stuck" if everyone has equal power. That person doesn't necessarily have to drive the conversation or even participate as long as things are moving along.

The fourth is operational reviews. In this meeting a functional unit should be presenting their progress, and their peers across other groups should provide feedback and suggestions. These should act as mini-board meetings for particular groups and should occur at least once a quarter for major teams.

There are fundamentally two different ways to make a decision between two people. "Position", meaning I am the most senior person, so I make the call and "Knowledge", meaning I am the person with the most knowledge about the situation. It's perfectly reasonable to overrule a junior person who is closer to the metal on something, but if you do so, you need to be responsible for understanding all of the inputs into that decision. Recognize though that you burn a certain amount of social capital each time you overrule a more junior person purely through position. If you do this over and over, instead of explaining the underlying why and shifting to a knowledge-based decision, you will eventually burn your best people out.

Ideally all the decisions being made in your organization should be made at the lowest necessary competence level, and are only bubbling up to you if your expertise is needed.

Peak performance

If you still feel like you aren't getting the peak performance from a team member that you expect, here's a final framework that can help. First, ask yourself whether this person is capable of doing the work you want them to do if their life depended on it. Is it a question of motivation or a question of capability.

If their life depended on it and they could do it, then that's on you as a leader not providing the proper motivation. Most of the time that's due to you not providing the larger story as to why their work is meaningful and the impact they will have. Per Goethe – "Dream no small dreams for these have no power to move the hearts of men."

If however, they would be unable to do it even if their life depended on it, then that is your mistake as a manager for expecting them to be able to. Someone's ability to do a particular task is called "task-relevant maturity" which essentially means how much experience does someone have doing this task.

If it is low, then you need to be incredibly structured and micromanage the employee as they accomplish a task. If they have done this task many times, then you can be far more laissez faire and just check in occasionally. This implies that your method of management is determined by the employee you're managing, not by your particular preference or style. This is also a great way to interview an executive, if you do reference checks on prior direct reports that they've had, ideally half of them will say she was a micromanager, and half will say she's very laid back.

Ideally, over time you are teaching your direct reports and extending them enough rope on decisions such that they are learning to make their own judgments over time. On any particular project or decision, you can sort it by the following variables: Your conviction (i.e., do you think you know the ideal right answer or best final product), and the consequence (i.e., if you make the wrong decision or ship an imperfect product, is there a catastrophic downside).

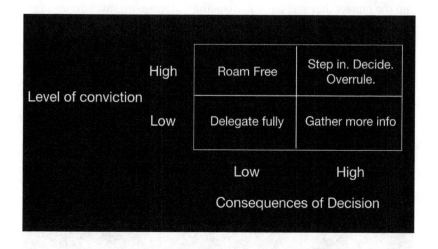

If both are low, then just delegate the project fully. If your conviction is high that you know the perfect solution, but your junior person disagrees, it's much better to let them go off and ship what they want to ship, as long as the consequences are low. You want to extend them rope to implement their own ideas and learn judgment on their own. On the other hand, if the consequences of a decision are high, you need to either have high conviction and overrule your junior teammate, or you need to ask them to go out and gather more information until you have high conviction about a decision. You can't wait until you get to 100% confidence on these types of decisions or else you will move too slowly, the ideal level is around 70%.

By extending junior people's ropes when the downside is low, they will gain task maturity and be able to handle more complex situations in the future. For example, one of my high-potential seed investments was going out for a Series A last year. Keith let me handle the negotiation for the round, which was the first time I was doing so on my own for that large of a round (I had only done seeds on my own to date). However, the consequence was relatively low here since we already had decent ownership in the company, so even if I botched it, it wasn't like we were going to end up entirely missing the company. In the end, I did totally botch the deal and we lost the A to another highly qualified firm for a variety of reasons. Keith extending me that rope taught me a lot and just a few months later I was able to close a promising Series A on my own.

You should be constantly expanding every team member's scope until they reach their breaking point. Everyone has one, no one can run the whole world. Your job is to discover everyone's individual breaking point. Then pare back and teach them how to handle more.

Here is the presentation [*bit.ly/training-keith*] Keith uses.

🎙 GitLab interview: GitLab's top strategies for a remote-first workplace

•• Watch the interview [*bit.ly/gitlab-remote-ceo*] and listen to the podcast episode on all major streaming platforms, including iTunes and Spotify (search for episode: The Remote Series with Sid Sijbrandij).

GitLab [*about.gitlab.com*] has been remote since its early days, and is now one of the biggest remote employers of all time. The company tripled in size during 2019 and currently employs 1,300 people across 67 countries and regions, with thousands more contributing to their open source project. According to CEO Sid Sibrandij [*twitter.com/sytses*], one of the key benefits of remote working is the ability to hire great people wherever they may be, without the risks or expense of owning an office.

But perks like that don't come for free — they're outputs of a system that's been carefully designed from the start.

Clearbit CEO Alex MacCaw and coach Matt Mochary sat down with Sid and GitLab's Head of Remote, Darren Murph [*twitter.com/darrenmurph*], to chat about their best practices for building a remote-first company. "One of the effects of [COVID] is that it's accelerated the global embrace of remote by at least ten years," Darren says. "It's time to start having more serious conversations about the best way to do things right."

GitLab believes every CEO should pay attention to three items in particular: creating social bonds through informal communication, rethinking process documentation, and staying very wary of the idea to go hybrid-remote when offices open back up.

Organize informal communication to encourage social bonding

In a physical office, people form bonds naturally, and companies even hire facility managers to create inviting spaces for casual run-ins. In a remote environment, however, physical proximity isn't an option, so social bonding needs constant nurturing. "You'll likely need to be a bit parental about it," Sid says.

With this in mind, GitLab organizes a diverse set of events and opportunities for connection, including:

- A week-long companywide offsite

- Visiting grants: a $150 stipend to cover travel costs for employees to visit one another

- An AirBnB in the Netherlands as a free-of-charge gathering space for teams

- Talent shows

- Short "take a break" calls with five non-work discussion topics

- Monthly retrospectives where the engineering team inspects and adapts their methods after completing an increment of work

Intentional social events, such as pizza parties or weekly hangouts, draw a line between work and play. "The social chatter can take any direction," Sid notes, "as long as you don't talk about the sprint in progress."

Social interactions are also baked into onboarding — GitLab arranges ten mandatory "coffee chats" for new employees that pair them up with a random colleague. Pairs are cross-functional, not within teams, to help prevent workplace silos. Socials, though optional, are regularly scheduled and boast high attendance rates.

Children of GitLab employees can also bond through "Juice Box Chats" on the Slack parenting channel, a digital space for parents working from home with kids. Juice Box Chats are for the whole family, and as Darren puts it, "You have kids that are in isolation but they're actually getting cultural exploration across six continents, which they probably couldn't even get if they were in school."

Being fully remote, with no office lease to answer to, frees up resources that GitLab can redirect to developing rich, intentional, informal communication channels that bring employees closer.

> For more tips on how to formalize informal communication, check out GitLab's list of 15 suggestions [*bit.ly/gitlab-comms*].

Enforce documentation and asynchronous communication

You're in trouble at GitLab if you refer to the company's 5,000-page handbook as "documentation." "It's not documentation," Sid says. "It's what we do."

GitLab works from a "handbook-first" perspective, so before any new process or project is implemented on any team, it's detailed in the handbook.

By contrast, many other companies craft proposals that are — maybe — later documented officially, almost as an afterthought … if thought of at all. "At every single company I've known outside of GitLab," Sid says, "the handbook is out of date and no one looks there."

This relentless focus on documenting processes — and their changes — isn't necessarily intuitive or easy to enforce and Sid needs to actively reinforce it throughout the organization. However, letting things slide raises the threat of slipping into workplace rhythms that aren't conducive to a remote-first environment. As Sid says, "Naturally, communication descends into meetings and synchronous communication."

For him, the continuous maintenance required for an up-to-date handbook is well worth the extra effort.

Stay away from hybrid-remote when offices reopen

There's been a lot of talk about companies moving to a hybrid-remote model as they reopen post-COVID. However, Sid warns against this approach and argues that companies should just go fully remote.

Half-and-half is not as simple as it sounds. As Sid says, "It's not like, 'Oh you need to do two things.' You need to do two things that *conflict*."

Because once a company reopens as a hybrid, some people will go back into the office and some people will continue to work remotely, depending on their roles and risk tolerance. Inevitably, this leads to two separate workstreams. "If the leadership is present at the office, it's clear which style is going to give you more information and more career opportunities," Sid says. "And the people who are remote will feel left out, and the most talented and ambitious people will leave."

Why, then, are offices reopening in the first place, especially when many companies have seen an increase in productivity while fully remote? "Is it a sunk cost fallacy because of the lease?" Sid asks. "Is it because they like what it affords them, the feeling of walking into the building they built, with the people that work for them? The only conclusion I can come to is that they think they need more informal communication. And I bet they do."

That is, employees crave more social connection, but going back to the office isn't the only way to get it. Sid says, "[People] don't want to go back to the office — they want to go back to informal communication with each other so they can restore these bonds." As GitLab shows, there are many ways for employees to connect. After all, if they live in the same city, they can get lunch together. It just doesn't need to be inside Git-Lab's office.

Sid provides a personal example. His extroverted wife loves her own workplace's culture and had never been keen on the idea of working remotely. But now that COVID has shut down her office, she's in no hurry for it to reopen. She grabs a daily boba tea with her colleagues and finds that taking Wednesdays off makes her more productive the rest of the week. Now that she's established her own informal communication channels, the downside of remote working has disappeared.

Remote work is effective — and investors are paying attention

The rise of COVID-19 has caused a sea change in the industry. The very investors who were once skeptical about GitLab's remote-first strategy — asking Sid to promise to drop it as soon as it stopped working — have become pro-remote.

"We found that your costs are way lower," Sid says. "Plus, you have 88% year over year retention, and you get better talent than any company we know. So we think this remote thing is a way to make companies work."

As the COVID headwinds continue to push back against a full reopening, now is a good time for CEOs to embrace remote work — and discover how it can make their teams even more effective.

If you're curious about how GitLab has succeeded with a global team and no office, take a look at the All-Remote section of the GitLab Handbook [*bit.ly/gitlab-allremote*].

It covers everything from embracing asynchronous workflows, communication styles and tips on running meetings, to remote hiring practices and global compensation strategies.

😃 Remote Happiness

Matt Mochary, who's coached many of the world's leading CEOs, has this to say about remote happiness.

With the advent of forced remote, many CEOs are finding that some of their team members are profoundly unhappy. They see this when valued team members choose to leave the 500+ person company and move to another job, most often to an organization with just a few people (early startup or investment firm), or to no job at all. This move often appears illogical. The person is giving up lots of compensation. The CEO often feels personally insulted, and certainly confused.

There is no need to be confused. The reasons are actually logical.

In this remote world, many people are feeling disconnected which in turn leads to sadness, often intense sadness (ie – depression). For those in this state, they know that something needs to change, but they are not sure what. Job is the activity that consumes most of their day, so they often assume that is where the cause lies. They believe that their disconnection comes from the fact that they are working at a "big company". If they leave for a small company, they will regain a sense of connection.

Unfortunately, they rarely do. Because their disconnection is not coming from the size of their company, but rather the way in which they are working remotely.

Most managers feel that they are not allowed to ask about a report's personal life, and therefore are unwilling to ask about the report's home environment and daily routines. This is a mistake. The manager is a coach whose role is to help their report unpack and solve the issues that the report faces, whether those issues appear in their work or personal world.

Therefore, as a manager, if you sense that one of your reports is unhappy or experiencing mental/emotional pain, ask them about it. Ask them about their home environment and daily routine. I posit that you will likely discover that they do not do or have at least one of the following:

- Get outside

- See other people that they know

- Exercise

- Have access to a consistently uninterrupted space to take Zoom calls

I posit that humans need 4 things to feel mentallly balanced:

- Connection to nature

- Connection to tribe

- Blood flow

- Uninterrupted work space

Pre-COVID, we could each achieve these to some degree simply by going to an office.

- We had to leave our residence each day to get to transportation which brought us to and from the office. By leaving our residence, we encountered outside air even if only briefly, and this created a connection to nature.

- We saw other people in the office who were familiar to us. They may not have been our best friends, but we knew them. We said hello and goodbye, maybe had lunch with them, maybe even met for drinks after work and shared an occasional laugh. This created connection to tribe.

- We had to physically walk to transport, which got our bodies moving a little bit and thus our blood flowing a bit. Many of us took advantage of being out by going to the gym and really getting our blood to flow.

- The office was geared for performance, with call booths, conference rooms or private offices for meetings and calls. Thus,we had uninterrupted work spaces.

We achieved these things unwittingly.

Rather than try to convince you that these elements create a feeling of peace and satisfaction, I simply challenge you to experiment with them.

While going to an in-person office naturally gave us each of these to a small degree, if we are intentional about creating them in a work-from-home environment, we can achieve them to a much higher degree, and therefore feel even greater personal satisfaction than we did when going to the office.

Here is how I do it.

Connection to nature

I take a 5-minute walk outside at the beginning of the day before I start work. And I take a 5-minute walk at the end of the day once I have stopped work. This not only creates a connection to nature by getting me into outside air, it also is a nice signal of the transition to and from work. Before the morning and after the evening transition, I do not allow myself to do work, leaving me space to focus on family and personal activities.

I also take breaks regularly throughout the day. I only schedule 25 – and 50-minute meetings, and I end all of them on time. This allows me a break to go to do one or more of the following:

* go to the bathroom

* get a drink of water

* get a snack

* get outside

* prepare for the next meeting

When I get outside (which I do at least once every 2 hours), I:

* Close my eyes and face the sun (even if it's cloudy) for 1 minute. This creates an intense and quick connection to nature.

* While doing so, I stretch my hip flexors while taking 5 deep breaths. This gets my blood flowing.

* Then I find my wife or one of my children and give them a 1-minute hug. (Truth be told, only my wife puts up with this. My kids top out at 10 seconds when they are willing to hug me at all.) This creates for me an intense and quick connection to tribe.

Connection to tribe

In addition to the 1-minute hugs mentioned above, I schedule in-person socially-distant gatherings at least once a week.

* I put zero effort into hosting. I am only willing to send an email stating the time and location of the gathering.

- Sometimes it is at an open-air restaurant/bar for a drink or meal. Sometimes it is on my patio where each guest must bring whatever they want to drink or eat.

- My intent is not to be rude, but rather to make organizing and hosting incredibly easy for me, increasing the likelihood that I will continue to do so.

- The purpose of these gatherings for me is laughter. I invite those with whom I am able to generate that laughter.

Blood flow

In addition to the short walks at the beginning and end of the day, and the 1-minute stretches during breaks, I also run on the treadmill. But rather than see how much I can do, I have experimented with how little I can do and still get the benefit of a feeling of peace and calm in my body that lasts for more than 24 hours. For me that time is 3 minutes at 4.0 speed. I end up running for 5 minutes just to be safe.

Once again, my goal is to make this step so easy (ie – short and slow) that there is no reason for me not to do it each day.

I should note that I often skip the morning walk in favor of the 5 minutes on the treadmill, because my treadmill is in an unattached garage, so I have to go outside to get to it. Thus, I am getting my connection to nature anyway.

Uninterrupted work space

I have converted a back room into a Zoom studio. It is far from the locus of kids' activities, and I am able to lock the door so that no one accidentally wanders in.

Many of your team members do not have a large enough home, or an unused room, to create such an uninterrupted space. The answer for them is either

- A co-working space outside the home.

- Rent a home in a cheaper part of the country where they can afford a much larger space.

- I recommend that the company give a rent stipend that can be used toward either a co-work space or the remote residence.

My wife and I have hired a homeschool teacher to be with our children. Many of your team members cannot afford to do this on their own. For them, you can:

- Change the culture in the company. Re-frame a child walking into a Zoom call as a welcome introduction of the team member's family to their co-workers. Ask the meeting owner to look forward to these moments as a way to increase team bonding by getting to know each other as humans.

- Do what Gitlab does and create Juicebox Zoom calls that bring families together for remote play dates throughout the day. And introduces them to children in a myriad of locations that they would otherwise never have access to.

- Encourage parents to partner with other families to create a microschool (hire a teacher jointly).

With these steps above, I feel connected, grounded and peaceful throughout the day. Even when I have back-to-back-to-back Zoom calls throughout the entire day, I feel energized as long as I actually take a break between each call, and actually get outside during those breaks.

There are other things that contribute to my sense of well-being. They are:

Desk set-up

- I have a standing desk. Because of it, my neck, back and body do not get sore or stiff. (Before I had a standing desk, I used a neck pillow with pressure knobs for a few minutes during breaks and at the end of the day to relieve the tension in my neck and back.)

- I have placed my desk directly in front of a window. This achieves two purposes:

  » It allows me to look outside at nature throughout the day. I also open the window to allow in fresh air when the weather cooperates. This gives me connection to nature.

  » The natural light on my face is akin to professional video lighting, allowing me to appear fully present during video calls.

Morning routine

- I follow Tim Ferriss's morning routine suggestion [*bit.ly/ ferrissAMroutine*].

  » Meditate for 10 minutes (while still in bed) using the Waking Up app.

  » Journal (while still in bed) using the 5-Minute Journal.

  » Make my bed.

  » Drink a large glass of water.

  » 5-minute run on the treadmill.

  » Every other day, I do push-ups using the Just 6 Weeks app.

- This 20-30 minute routine invigorates me and launches me with energy and clarity into the tasks of the day.

Meals

- I try to eat every meal and snack sitting outside.

Entertainment

- I try (with decent success) to not look at an electronic device for entertainment. This means that I no longer look at my phone to view news, Twitter, YouTube, etc.

- Without electronic entertainment, I am forced to do other activities during non-work times. I end up:

  » Sitting outside and staring at the leaves blowing in the wind (intense connection to nature)

  » Talking with my wife (connection to tribe)

  » Talking and playing with my kids (connection to tribe)

  » Reading a paper book (soothing)

- All of these activities bring me a sense of peace, whereas looking at my phone or a screen never did.

Time away

- I do not work at all on the weekends, guaranteeing myself 2 days of rejuvenation each week. And I take a long weekend with my family once every few months.

  » Plaid recently looked at vacation days and found that their team members weren't taking them … at all. So, Plaid scheduled two 4-day weekends for 2H20. During these long weekends, no one at Plaid is allowed to work. (Of course, Plaid can't stop the sales team from responding to emails. But hopefully they will be doing so from a nice location.)

» I recommend that you do the same.

Please think of these suggestions as things to experiment with. There are many other ways to create connection to nature, connection to tribe, blood flow and uninterrupted work space.

Find the ways that work for you. Simply make sure that you do them every day, and several times each day.

And as a Manager, make sure that your reports are doing so as well. If you do, I posit that you and your team members will retain a lasting sense of connection, peace and well-being. And your team members will therefore stay with the company.

Acknowledgements

I am deeply grateful to my teachers: Matt Mochary, The Conscious Leadership Foundation, Kiki Samuels, Eric Feldman, Justin Kan, Anand Sharma, Keith Rabois, Sid Sibrandij, JD Ross, Amit Vasudev, Luke Whiting, Sasha Mackinnon, and countless more.

I am also deeply grateful for the Clearbit team, who helped revise and improve a lot of the practices contained in this book.

A huge debt of gratitude goes to Matt Sornson, co-founder of Clearbit, without whom this book wouldn't exist. Matt co-hosted the book's podcast, read drafts, encouraged me, and ultimately made this project a lot of fun.

Lastly, I would like to thank everyone who reviewed each chapter, including:

Ye Cheng, Florin Sirghea, Ricardo Clérigo, Phil Freo, Francisco H. de Mello, José Akle, Matt Dalley, Bay Gross, Tim Ahmann, Dasha Maggio, Eduardo Rocha, Siddharth Mohan, Mitch Cde Baca, Kjetil Holmefjord, Matthias Richard, Roberto Barbosa Oliveira, Rory Madden, Ulrich Sossou, Rohan Goel, Adam Albarghouthi, Rajaraman Santhanam, Steve Quatrani, Will Morgan, Simon Turner, Vicente Plata, Sam Morgan, Dave Brown, Mogens Møller, Jonathan Cutrell, Matthew Ford, Luiz Argenta, Sheree Atcheson, Rohan Williams, Marit Nexus, Charles Williamson, Roberto Braga, Jorge Davila, Stas Kulesh, Nicole Anne Dy, Mike Palmer, Marcelo Fujimoto, Cody J. Landstrom, Josh Tucholski, Max Olson, Kacy Fortner, Alvaro Barbosa, Philip Thomas, Rahul Desai, Jason Past, Thilo Konzok, Alex Booker, Magda Meza, Sean D., Stephen M. Walker II, Vlad Ciurca, Angie Lal, Andrew Forbes, Dominik Woj, Aleksandar Dragojlović, Randy Pratt, Tiffany Zhong, Yuriy Dybskiy, Marcel Wösle, Jake Fuentes, Oswald Yeo, Roberto Mascarenhas Braga, Alexandre Kantjas, Aaron Epperson, Paul Rieger, Val Agostino, Sebastian Alvarado, Eric Feldman, Yoni Elbaz, Yasmin Razavi, Osama Khan, Lalit Patel, Piyush

Patel, Katsuya Noguchi, Dominic Jodoin, Ionut Ciobotaru, Mike Weiss, Vindhya C., Nirant K., Samyak Pandya, Tom Leitch, Ben Moore, Arpit Rai, Andrei Serban, Abi Tyas Tunggal, Gabriel Lim, Beau Lebens, James Costa, Chanpory Rith, Luke Segars, Will Wearing, Gautam Kedia, Hampus Jakobsson, Dasha Barannik, Petr Hlubina, Jorge Izquierdo, Dominic Chapman, Mandar Gokhale, Pablo Vallejo, Adam Waxman, Matt Woods, Anthony Sexton, Luciano Tavares, Jigar Patel, Tina Phillips, Sanjay Dastoor, Benjamin Mora, Michael Molesky, and Lj Kyser.

About the Author

Alex MacCaw

Alex MacCaw is the founder of Clearbit.

Follow @maccaw on Twitter.